LINUX INTERNALS SIMPLIFIED

Md Haris Iqbal, Kundan Kumar, Prasad Paple

Dedicated to everyone who has contributed to the development of the Linux Kernel.

I would like to thank my parents, wife Neha and my cute daughters for all their time and encouragement. Thanks to my knowledgeable seniors and colleagues for innumerable technical discussions. Thanks to Kurumurthy, Shubham, Sanjib, Haris, Sreeni, Satbir for always encouraging me.
- Kundan Kumar

I would like to thank my parents, and my siblings; for their continuous support and love. I would also like to thank all my friends for being there for me at different stages of my life; Especially Kundan, Ashwin, Nushafreen, Madhuri, Debarghyo, Pamela, and Taqi.
- Md Haris Iqbal

I would like to thank my parents and wife Padma for their love and support.I would like to express my gratitude to all my friends especially Kundan, Kislaya and Surendra for their encouragement.
- Prasad Paple

Acknowledgment

Our thanks are due to Nushafreen Palsetia, for giving her valuable time to review the chapters and provide useful feedback and corrections.

Our thanks are due Dr. Keshava Munegowda, for helping us with the publishing formalities.

Table of Contents

Preface

When we first started learning about the Linux kernel, we adopted an empirical approach; diving directly into the code, experimenting with minor changes, basically trying to develop a better understanding of the kernel by reverse engineering the code. When faced with complex data structures or designs that did not speak to us directly through the code, we searched for related material to get a better understanding of what was going on. It occurred to us that there might be a way to make this process simpler for someone looking to learn about the implementation of the kernel.

It seemed to us that a good starting point for anyone delving into Linux internals for the first time, a reference point, which provided a foundation of overall design of the major modules along with tools for following through with the code, would be extremely useful. This is how the idea of this book was born.

This book aims to provide a good high level introduction of how modules are organized, how they communicate with each other, how the code execution flows and so on; a consolidated knowledge trove of basic points in the Linux kernel which would encourage a beginner to do a deep dive by providing enough knowledge of the entire system to take the next step.

The book also strives to bridge the gap between abstract operating system concepts and actual implementation of these in a production ready, industry hardened system code. A beginner armed with theoretical knowledge of different operating system concepts will be able to relate to the design and code examples presented in this book. We hope this book helps the reader to develop a clearer picture of "how things work" inside the Linux kernel machinery.

About the book

"Linux internals simplified" is a book which discusses the basics of Linux kernel internals in a code driven approach. It picks the major subsystems of the kernel which are important, and tries to simplify its internal working and data structures. As such, this book is aimed at engineers who wish to start learning about the Linux kernel.

This book assumes that the reader is well versed with the general programming constructs and has a good knowledge of C programming language. Linux kernel is mostly written in C, except places where one can find assembly language. Hence, it goes without saying that even after going through this book, when the reader would eventually dive into the Linux kernel code by himself, a strong knowledge of C would make this task easier.

There are several points which the reader of this book should be aware of.

1. This book discusses the code and design of the kernel version 5.0.0.
2. While discussing architecture specific code, we have chosen to stick with the x86 architecture.
3. Names of functions and data structures which are taken right from the code are mentioned in double quotes.

Chapter 1 Linux kernel compilation and modification

In this chapter we shall see Linux kernel compilation from its source code. We are using Ubuntu and using the latest kernel available now. In this chapter we will go through the kernel source code location in upstream, kernel compilation procedure and kernel configuration file. We will also deal with the kernel images which are generated as a result of the compilation process.

Mostly we will use Ubuntu for our work done in this book.

Kernel source code

We can download the latest Linux kernel source code from https://www.kernel.org/

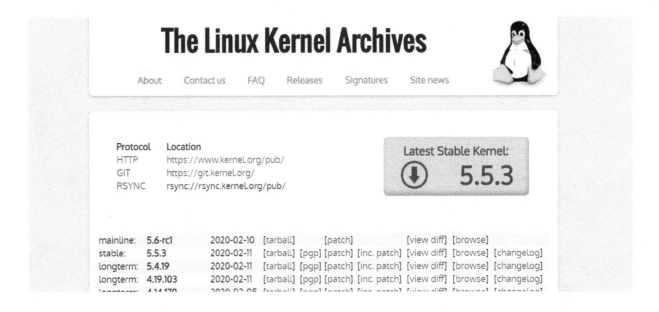

We will download the latest stable kernel source code tarball and start compiling it.

Let us download the current available stable kernel version of 5.5.3 using "wget"

```
root@x-virtual-machine:~/latest_stable_kernel# wget
https://cdn.kernel.org/pub/linux/kernel/v5.x/linux-
5.5.3.tar.xz
```

```
--2020-02-13 18:11:13--
https://cdn.kernel.org/pub/linux/kernel/v5.x/linux-
5.5.3.tar.xz
Resolving cdn.kernel.org (cdn.kernel.org)...
2a04:4e42:46::432, 199.232.37.176
Connecting to cdn.kernel.org
(cdn.kernel.org)|2a04:4e42:46::432|:443... failed: Network
is unreachable.
Connecting to cdn.kernel.org
(cdn.kernel.org)|199.232.37.176|:443... connected.
HTTP request sent, awaiting response... 200 OK
Length: 110706004 (106M) [application/x-xz]
Saving to: 'linux-5.5.3.tar.xz'

linux-5.5.3.tar.xz  100%[==================>] 105.58M
8.91MB/s    in 12s

2020-02-13 18:11:29 (9.02 MB/s) - 'linux-5.5.3.tar.xz'
saved [110706004/110706004]

root@x-virtual-machine:~/latest_stable_kernel#
```

Let's extract the kernel source code :
```
root@x-virtual-machine:~/latest_stable_kernel# tar xf
linux-5.5.3.tar.xz

root@x-virtual-machine:~/latest_stable_kernel# ls

linux-5.5.3  linux-5.5.3.tar.xz
```

Kernel configuration file

A Linux kernel code is associated with many configuration flags. Using these configuration flags, a kernel can cater to various needs. By changing these configuration flags, the same kernel code can be compiled for a watch, embedded boards, servers, mobile phones etc.

For a booted Ubuntu the configuration file is present in /boot directory

```
root@x-virtual-machine:~# ls /boot/
config-4.18.0-15-generic          memtest86+.elf
config-5.0.0-050000-generic       memtest86+_multiboot.bin
config-5.0.0-25-generic           System.map-4.18.0-15-
generic
config-5.3.0-28-generic           System.map-5.0.0-050000-
generic
grub                              System.map-5.0.0-25-
generic
initrd.img-4.18.0-15-generic      System.map-5.3.0-28-
generic
initrd.img-5.0.0-050000-generic   vmlinuz-4.18.0-15-generic
initrd.img-5.0.0-25-generic       vmlinuz-5.0.0-050000-
generic
initrd.img-5.3.0-28-generic       vmlinuz-5.0.0-25-generic
memtest86+.bin                    vmlinuz-5.3.0-28-generic
```

Let's see the content of a config file :

```
...
#
# IRQ subsystem
#
CONFIG_GENERIC_IRQ_PROBE=y
CONFIG_GENERIC_IRQ_SHOW=y
CONFIG_GENERIC_IRQ_EFFECTIVE_AFF_MASK=y
CONFIG_GENERIC_PENDING_IRQ=y
CONFIG_GENERIC_IRQ_MIGRATION=y
CONFIG_GENERIC_IRQ_CHIP=y
CONFIG_IRQ_DOMAIN=y
CONFIG_IRQ_DOMAIN_HIERARCHY=y
CONFIG_GENERIC_MSI_IRQ=y
...
```

. . .

The configuration file has the flags mentioned with their respective values. Linux kernel source code and a working configuration file is enough to compile a kernel.

Kernel Compilation

We will go to the location where we have unzipped the kernel source code.

At the same location we copy the config to .config :

```
root@x-vm:~/latest_stable_kernel/linux-5.5.3# cp
/boot/config-5.0.0-25-generic .config
```

Let's find and modify print statement :

```
Feb 13 18:59:32 x-virtual-machine kernel: [    0.000000]
KERNEL supported cpus:
```

This belongs to file arch/x86/kernel/cpu/common.c
Let's modify this to

pr_info("KERNEL supported cpus: !!! CHECK THE MODIFICATION !!!\n");

Now we can make the Linux kernel image using the "make" tool :
Commands which make and install the kernel with modules are as follows :

```
root@x-vm:~/latest_stable_kernel/linux-5.5.3# make
root@x-vm:~/latest_stable_kernel/linux-5.5.3# make
modules_install
root@x-vm:~/latest_stable_kernel/linux-5.5.3# make install
```

"make modules_install" creates a directory in "/lib/modules" :

```
root@x-vm:/lib/modules/5.5.3# pwd
/lib/modules/5.5.3
```

Also **"make install"** updates /boot/ directory, creates initrd and copies kernel image : vmlinuz

In short if we see the steps to compile and install Linux kernel :
1. extract kernel
2. switch to the directory
3. copy the config to .config
4. make
5. make modules_install
6. make install

After this the grub entry is also modified to include the latest kernel compilation.

Other helpful commands

The command "make help" tells various binaries which can be generated in the kernel directory.

make mrproper -- This command cleans up the entire kernel directory and removes the intermediate files. This command also cleans the ".config" file and for the next rebuild you need to generate the ".config" again.

make oldconfig -- This command is used when your kernel source code is new, and the config file was generated using an old kernel.

Modifying the configurations

The modification of the configuration can be done using the "make menuconfig" tool.

"make menuconfig" command opens up a GUI for modifying the configuration, as shown below.

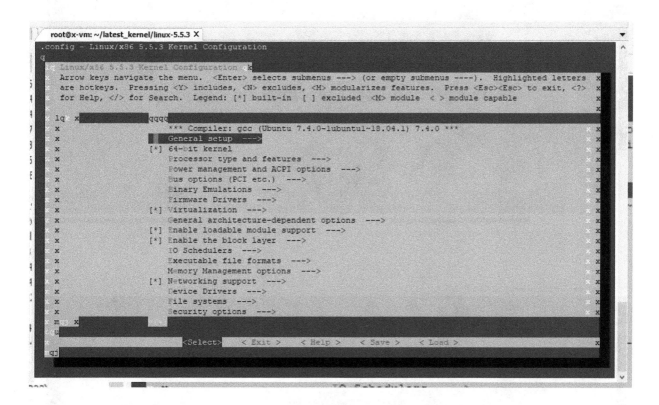

<Enter> on a selected field goes down the configuration tree.
<Esc><Esc> two times comes up the tree.

"/" press will open up the search prompt. The search prompt can be used to search for a specific parameter. Following diagrams illustrate the search ways :

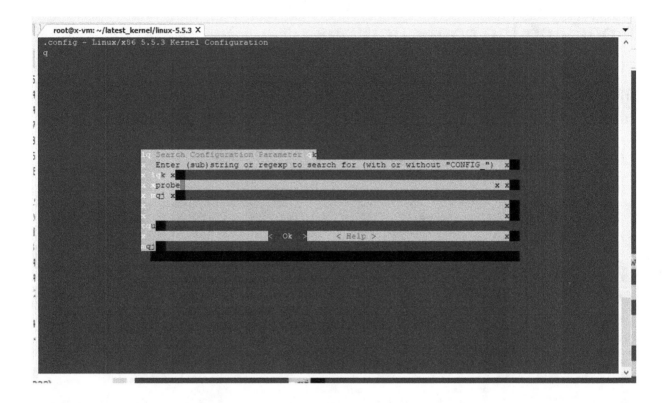

Linux kernel Images

As a result of the above compilation process the bzImage (Kernel binary) is generated. Let's see the size of this binary:

```
root@x-vm:~/latest_kernel/linux-5.5.3# ls -lh
arch/x86/boot/bzImage
-rw-r--r-- 1 root root 8.9M Feb 14 23:01
arch/x86/boot/bzImage
```

We can see that the entire kernel Image is contained in 8.9 MB only.

Let's see the output of file command for this kernel image :

```
root@x-vm:~/latest_kernel/linux-5.5.3# file
./arch/x86/boot/bzImage
./arch/x86/boot/bzImage: Linux kernel x86 boot executable
bzImage, version 5.5.3 (root@x-vm) #1 SMP Fri Feb 14
19:02:56 IST 2020, RO-rootFS, swap
_dev 0x8, Normal VGA
```

Let's check for the symbol table in this kernel image:

```
root@x-vm:~/latest_kernel/linux-5.5.3# objdump -T
./arch/x86/boot/bzImage
objdump: ./arch/x86/boot/bzImage: Warning: Ignoring section
flag IMAGE_SCN_MEM_NOT_PAGED in section .bss

./arch/x86/boot/bzImage:      file format pei-x86-64

objdump: ./arch/x86/boot/bzImage: not a dynamic object
DYNAMIC SYMBOL TABLE:
no symbols
```

This clearly says that in this kernel image the symbols are not present. If we want to create a kernel image with the symbol table then we need to give the command:

```
root@x-vm:~/latest_kernel/linux-5.5.3# make vmlinux
```

This generates a kernel image : vmlinux with the symbol table info

```
root@x-vm:~/latest_kernel/linux-5.5.3#  file vmlinux
vmlinux: ELF 64-bit LSB executable, x86-64, version 1
(SYSV), statically linked,
BuildID[sha1]=ae9f5490b109b8fe8447ec7f1e580c0fa3d9a34e,
with deb
ug_info, not stripped

root@x-vm:~/latest_kernel/linux-5.5.3# objdump -t vmlinux |
more
vmlinux:     file format elf64-x86-64

SYMBOL TABLE:
ffffffff81000000 l    d  .text  0000000000000000 .text
ffffffff82000000 l    d  .rodata         0000000000000000
.rodata
ffffffff8246ca80 l    d  .pci_fixup      0000000000000000
.pci_fixup
ffffffff8246f9e0 l    d  .tracedata      0000000000000000
.tracedata
ffffffff8246fa58 l    d  __ksymtab       0000000000000000
__ksymtab
ffffffff8247f814 l    d  __ksymtab_gpl   0000000000000000
__ksymtab_gpl
ffffffff8248ff30 l    d  __ksymtab_strings
0000000000000000 __ksymtab_strings
ffffffff824c7be0 l    d  __init_rodata   0000000000000000
__init_rodata
ffffffff824c7e70 l    d  __param         0000000000000000
__param
ffffffff824cafa8 l    d  __modver        0000000000000000
__modver
ffffffff824cb030 l    d  __ex_table      0000000000000000
__ex_table
ffffffff824ccc50 l    d  .notes 0000000000000000 .notes
ffffffff82600000 l    d  .data  0000000000000000 .data
ffffffff82852f40 l    d  __bug_table     0000000000000000
__bug_table
```

We can see that the symbol table information is present in the vmlinux file.

...

...

Size of vmlinux :

```
root@x-vm:~/latest_kernel/linux-5.5.3# ls -lh vmlinux
-rwxr-xr-x 1 root root 665M Feb 14 23:01 vmlinux
```

Chapter 2   Linux Hacking Tools

In this chapter we will see various Linux kernel hacking techniques. These tools make it easy to debug/trace a live Linux system.
We can avoid the Linux Kernel compilation if we use these tools :

Ftrace

Ftrace tool can be used to trace the kernel functions.
1. It can be used to dump all the kernel functions which got executed while tracing was enabled.
2. It can be used for generating function graphs of a kernel function.
3. It can be used for profiling purposes, where we can see the time consumed for execution by each kernel function.

The Ftrace support is built-in in the Linux kernel. The kernel configuration flags which shall be enabled for the Ftrace are :
```
CONFIG_FUNCTION_TRACER
CONFIG_FUNCTION_GRAPH_TRACER
CONFIG_STACK_TRACER
CONFIG_DYNAMIC_FTRACE
```

Let's see the tracing directory of Ftrace :
```
root@x-vm:~# cd /sys/kernel/debug/tracing
root@x-vm:/sys/kernel/debug/tracing# ls
available_events              events
README                       snapshot              trace_pipe
available_filter_functions   free_buffer
saved_cmdlines               stack_max_size        trace_stat
available_tracers                 function_profile_enabled
saved_cmdlines_size   stack_trace          tracing_cpumask
buffer_percent                hwlat_detector
saved_tgids           stack_trace_filter
tracing_max_latency
buffer_size_kb                    instances
set_event             synthetic_events      tracing_on
buffer_total_size_kb          kprobe_events
set_event_pid         timestamp_mode        tracing_thresh
```

```
current_tracer                  kprobe_profile
set_ftrace_filter      trace                  uprobe_events
dynamic_events              max_graph_depth
set_ftrace_notrace     trace_clock         uprobe_profile
dyn_ftrace_total_info       options
set_ftrace_pid         trace_marker
enabled_functions              per_cpu
set_graph_function     trace_marker_raw
error_log                  printk_formats
set_graph_notrace      trace_options
```

Here

1. available_tracers : tells various ways of tracing given by ftrace
2. available_filter_functions : tells all the kernel functions which can be traced
3. current_tracer : this is used to select the type of tracing.
3. trace : this is the file where the generated trace will be dumped
4. max_graph_depth : used to set the depth while using the function graph tracing
5. tracing_on : echo 1 to this file starts the tracing.

Now let's dump all the kernel functions for a particular time. For this we use the function tracer :

Steps for switching tracing ON and OFF

Steps : Switch ON the tracing
1. cd /sys/kernel/debug/tracing
2. cat available_tracers
```
hwlat blk mmiotrace function_graph wakeup_dl wakeup_rt wakeup
function nop
```
3. echo function > current_tracer
4. echo 1 > tracing_on

Wait for some time or execute a test case for which you need the kernel function output.

Copy the trace file to some other directory

Steps to Switch OFF the tracing and clean trace file :

1. echo 0 > tracing_on
2. echo nop > current_tracer
3. cat /dev/null > trace

This is the output which we get as a **trace file:**

```
# tracer: function
#
# entries-in-buffer/entries-written: 368738/3519733    #P:8
#
#                              _-----=> irqs-off
#                             / _----=> need-resched
#                            | / _----=> hardirq/softirq
#                            || / _--=> preempt-depth
#                            ||| /     delay
#           TASK-PID   CPU#  ||||    TIMESTAMP  FUNCTION
#              | |       |   ||||       |          |
         <idle>-0     [006] d... 16951.398997: smp_apic_timer_interrupt <-
apic_timer_interrupt
         <idle>-0     [006] d... 16951.398998: irq_enter <-smp_apic_timer_interrupt
         <idle>-0     [006] d... 16951.398998: rcu_irq_enter <-irq_enter
         <idle>-0     [006] d... 16951.398998: rcu_dynticks_eqs_exit <-rcu_irq_enter
         <idle>-0     [006] d... 16951.398999: tick_irq_enter <-irq_enter
         <idle>-0     [006] d... 16951.398999: tick_check_oneshot_broadcast_this_cpu
<-tick_irq_enter
         <idle>-0     [006] d... 16951.398999: ktime_get <-tick_irq_enter
         <idle>-0     [006] d... 16951.399000: update_ts_time_stats <-tick_irq_enter
         <idle>-0     [006] d... 16951.399000: nr_iowait_cpu <-update_ts_time_stats
         <idle>-0     [006] d... 16951.399001: _local_bh_enable <-irq_enter
         <idle>-0     [006] d.h. 16951.399004: hrtimer_interrupt <-
smp_apic_timer_interrupt
         <idle>-0     [006] d.h. 16951.399004: _raw_spin_lock_irqsave <-
hrtimer_interrupt
         <idle>-0     [006] d.h. 16951.399005: ktime_get_update_offsets_now <-
hrtimer_interrupt
         <idle>-0     [006] d.h. 16951.399005: __hrtimer_run_queues <-
hrtimer_interrupt
```

If we see more in the trace file, we can see that it is capturing all the interrupts happening.

```
        <idle>-0       [005] d... 16965.237542: irq_enter <-do_IRQ
        <idle>-0       [005] d... 16965.237542: rcu_irq_enter <-irq_enter
        <idle>-0       [005] d... 16965.237543: rcu_dynticks_eqs_exit <-rcu_irq_enter
        <idle>-0       [005] d... 16965.237543: tick_irq_enter <-irq_enter
        <idle>-0       [005] d... 16965.237543: tick_check_oneshot_broadcast_this_cpu
<-tick_irq_enter
        <idle>-0       [005] d... 16965.237543: ktime_get <-tick_irq_enter
        <idle>-0       [005] d... 16965.237544: update_ts_time_stats <-tick_irq_enter
        <idle>-0       [005] d... 16965.237544: nr_iowait_cpu <-update_ts_time_stats
        <idle>-0       [005] d... 16965.237544: _local_bh_enable <-irq_enter
        <idle>-0       [005] d.h. 16965.237545: handle_edge_irq <-do_IRQ
        <idle>-0       [005] d.h. 16965.237545: _raw_spin_lock <-handle_edge_irq
        <idle>-0       [005] d.h. 16965.237546: irq_may_run <-handle_edge_irq
        <idle>-0       [005] d.h. 16965.237546: irq_chip_ack_parent <-handle_edge_irq
        <idle>-0       [005] d.h. 16965.237547: apic_ack_edge <-irq_chip_ack_parent
        <idle>-0       [005] d.h. 16965.237547: apic_chip_data.part.18 <-apic_ack_edge
```

Generating function graph of a kernel function

We can also use ftrace for generating function graphs of any kernel function. We will show the generation of function_graph for _do_fork kernel function.

Steps for generating function graph using Ftrace :

Steps : Switch ON the tracing

```
cd /sys/kernel/debug/tracing
echo function_graph > current_tracer
echo _do_fork > set_graph_function
echo 10 > max_graph_depth
echo 1 > tracing_on
```

As a test case run any C program
```
./a.out
```

Steps to Switch OFF the tracing and clean trace file
```
cp trace ~/do_fork_trace
```

```
echo 0 > tracing_on
echo > set_graph_function
echo 0 > max_graph_depth
cat /dev/null > trace
```

We can see the graph generated in the trace file :

```
# tracer: function_graph
#
# CPU   DURATION                  FUNCTION CALLS
# |      |   |                     |   |   |   |
 0)                  |  _do_fork() {
 0)                  |    copy_process.part.37() {
 0)   0.498 us       |      _raw_spin_lock_irq();
 0)                  |      recalc_sigpending() {
 0)   0.170 us       |        recalc_sigpending_tsk();
 0)   0.831 us       |      }
 0)   0.225 us       |      tsk_fork_get_node();
 0)                  |      kmem_cache_alloc_node() {
...
...
...

 0)   0.170 us       |        copy_semundo();
 0)                  |        dup_fd() {
 0)                  |          kmem_cache_alloc() {
 0)                  |            _cond_resched() {
 0)   0.177 us       |              rcu_all_qs();
 0)   0.523 us       |            }
 0)   0.170 us       |            should_failslab();
 0)   1.305 us       |          }

...
...

 0)                  |        copy_fs_struct() {
 0)                  |          kmem_cache_alloc() {

...
```

```
...
0)                    |            mm_init() {
0)    0.171 us        |               __init_rwsem();
0)                    |               pgd_alloc() {
0)                    |                  __get_free_pages() {
0)                    |                     alloc_pages_current() {
```

Isn't it nice to see through the graph of the "_do_fork()" function :)

Similarly, we can generate function graphs for all the kernel functions.

Kprobes

Kprobes are another powerful tool which can help us in sniffing through the kernel functions, as and when they get executed.

Kprobes can be applied to any kernel function. A kprobe associated with a given kernel function gets executed just prior to the kernel function call. Kprobes are also based on the kernel support for it.

We will see an example kernel module which once executed puts a probe on the "blk_mq_make_request()" function. As long as this module is inserted, anytime "blk_mq_make_request()" function gets called first the kprobe is called then "blk_mq_make_request()" is called.

"struct pt_regs" structure holds the values of all general-purpose registers. Also in x86_64 we see that kernel functions get the first 6 arguments in rdi, rsi, rdx, rcx, r8, r9 registers.

Taking a look at the "blk_mq_make_request()" function in the file "block/blk-mq.c":
```
static blk_qc_t blk_mq_make_request(struct request_queue
*q, struct bio *bio)
```

We see that rdi and rsi are the registers where "request_queue" and "bio" structures are passed as parameters.

Sample Linux module :

```c
/*kprobe_example.c*/
#include <linux/kernel.h>
#include <linux/module.h>
#include <linux/kprobes.h>
#include <linux/kallsyms.h>
#include <linux/sched.h>
#include <linux/blk_types.h>
#include <linux/genhd.h>
#include <linux/blkdev.h>
/* For each probe you need to allocate a kprobe structure
*/
static struct kprobe kp;

/* kprobe pre_handler: called just before the probed
instruction is executed */
int handler_pre(struct kprobe *p, struct pt_regs *regs)
{
        static int x = 0;
        struct bio *bio_ptr = NULL;
        struct request_queue *rq_ptr = NULL;
        if (x%1000 == 0)
        {
                // first 6 arguments in rdi, rsi, rdx, rcx,
r8, r9
                printk("MY pre_handler:rdi=0x%08lx,
rsi=0x%08lx, rdx=0x%08lx\n",
                        regs->di, regs->si, regs->dx);
                rq_ptr = (struct request_queue *)regs->di;
                if(rq_ptr) {
                        printk("queue_depth = %d\n",rq_ptr-
>queue_depth);
                }
                else
                        printk("q ptr is NULL\n");
```

```
                bio_ptr = (struct bio *)regs->si;
                if (bio_ptr && bio_ptr->bi_disk ) {
                        printk("disk_name = %s\n", bio_ptr-
>bi_disk->disk_name);
                        printk("disk_ptr =
0x%08lx\n",bio_ptr->bi_disk);
                }
                printk("MY pre_handler: p->addr=0x%p,
eip=%lx, eflags=0x%lx\n",
                        p->addr, regs->ip, regs->flags);
                dump_stack();
        }
        x++;
        return 0;
}


/* kprobe post_handler: called after the probed instruction
is executed */
void handler_post(struct kprobe *p, struct pt_regs *regs,
unsigned long flags)
{
        static int y = 0;
        struct bio *bio_ptr;
        if (y%1000 == 0) {
        printk("MY post_handler: p->addr=0x%p,
eflags=0x%lx\n",
                p->addr, regs->flags);
        }
        y++;
}
int handler_fault(struct kprobe *p, struct pt_regs *regs,
int trapnr)
{
        printk("MY fault_handler: p->addr=0x%p, trap #%dn",
                p->addr, trapnr);
        /* Return 0 because we don't handle the fault. */
        return 0;
}
```

```
int init_module(void)
{
        int ret;
        kp.pre_handler = handler_pre;
        kp.post_handler = handler_post;
        kp.fault_handler = handler_fault;
        kp.addr = (kprobe_opcode_t*)
kallsyms_lookup_name("blk_mq_make_request");
        /* register the kprobe now */
        if (!kp.addr) {
                printk("Couldn't find %s to plant
kprobe\n", "_do_fork");
                return -1;
        }
        if ((ret = register_kprobe(&kp) < 0)) {
                printk("register_kprobe failed, returned
%d\n", ret);
                return -1;
        }
        printk("kprobe registered\n");
        return 0;
}
void cleanup_module(void)
{
        unregister_kprobe(&kp);
        printk("kprobe unregistered\n");
}


MODULE_LICENSE("GPL");
```

Makefile for this module :

```
obj-m+=kprobe_example.o
KDIR=/lib/modules/$(shell uname -r)/build
all:
        $(MAKE) -C $(KDIR) SUBDIRS=$(PWD) modules
```

```
clean:
        rm -rf *.o *.ko *.mod.* .c* .t* .*.cmd
.tmp_versions
```

After running "make", we inserted the kprobe_example.ko module using insmod

```
root@x-server:~/signal# insmod kprobe_example.ko
```

Listed the kprobe_example module using lsmod

```
root@x-server:~/signal# lsmod | grep kprobe_example
kprobe_example          16384  0
```

After the kprobe we can uninstall the module using rmmod

```
root@x-server:~/signal# rmmod kprobe_example
```

You can check the dump_stack statements getting hit whenever a call to "blk_mq_make_request()" is made.

```
kernel: [519941.544476] kprobe registered
kernel: [519945.038678] MY
pre_handler:rdi=0xffff955a2c786868, rsi=0xffff955a338e8600,
rdx=0x00000000
kernel: [519945.038688] queue_depth = 256
kernel: [519945.038695] disk_name = sda
kernel: [519945.038703] disk_ptr = 0xffff955a37c80000
kernel: [519945.038713] MY pre_handler: p-
>addr=0x000000001ecd1ebc, eip=ffffffff9dea21a1,
eflags=0x246
kernel: [519945.038725] CPU: 6 PID: 17239 Comm:
kworker/u97:2 Tainted: G          OE      5.0.0-050000-
generic #201903032031
kernel: [519945.038734] Hardware name: Dell Inc. PowerEdge
R730/072T6D, BIOS 2.3.4 11/08/2016
kernel: [519945.038753] Workqueue: writeback wb_workfn
(flush-8:0)
kernel: [519945.038769] Call Trace:
kernel: [519945.038791]  dump_stack+0x63/0x8a
```

```
kernel: [519945.038814]   handler_pre+0xa9/0x100
[kprobe_example]
kernel: [519945.038830]   ? blk_mq_make_request+0x1/0x4e0
kernel: [519945.038849]   kprobe_ftrace_handler+0x8f/0xf0
kernel: [519945.038866]   ?
blk_mq_try_issue_directly+0x2d0/0x2d0
kernel: [519945.038881]   ? generic_make_request+0x19e/0x400
kernel: [519945.038897]   ftrace_ops_list_func+0xc7/0x160
kernel: [519945.038925]   ftrace_regs_call+0x5/0x72
kernel: [519945.038959]   ? jbd2_journal_stop+0xf2/0x3f0
kernel: [519945.038973]   ?
blk_mq_try_issue_directly+0x2d0/0x2d0
kernel: [519945.038997]   ? blk_mq_make_request+0x1/0x4e0
kernel: [519945.039020]   blk_mq_make_request+0x5/0x4e0
kernel: [519945.039035]   generic_make_request+0x19e/0x400
kernel: [519945.039052]   ? blk_mq_make_request+0x5/0x4e0
kernel: [519945.039063]   ? generic_make_request+0x19e/0x400
kernel: [519945.039101]   submit_bio+0x49/0x140
kernel: [519945.039115]   ? ext4_io_submit+0x5/0x60
kernel: [519945.039131]   ? submit_bio+0x5/0x140
kernel: [519945.039153]   ext4_io_submit+0x4d/0x60
kernel: [519945.039170]   ext4_writepages+0x6b1/0xef0
kernel: [519945.039183]   ? function_graph_enter+0xcc/0x120
kernel: [519945.039228]   ? ftrace_graph_caller+0x78/0xb0
kernel: [519945.039249]   ?
page_writeback_cpu_online+0x20/0x20
kernel: [519945.039288]   ? ext4_writepages+0x4/0xef0
kernel: [519945.039319]   do_writepages+0x41/0xd0
kernel: [519945.039331]   ? ext4_writepages+0x5/0xef0
kernel: [519945.039343]   ? do_writepages+0x41/0xd0
kernel: [519945.039358]   ? do_writepages+0x5/0xd0
kernel: [519945.039369]   ? __writeback_inodes_wb+0x67/0xb0
kernel: [519945.039402]
__writeback_single_inode+0x40/0x350
kernel: [519945.039414]   ? wbc_detach_inode+0x190/0x190
kernel: [519945.039425]   ? __writeback_inodes_wb+0x67/0xb0
kernel: [519945.039441]   ? prepare_ftrace_return+0x5c/0x80
kernel: [519945.039466]   writeback_sb_inodes+0x211/0x500
```

```
kernel: [519945.039540]    __writeback_inodes_wb+0x67/0xb0
kernel: [519945.039571]    wb_writeback+0x25f/0x2f0
kernel: [519945.039620]    wb_workfn+0x32c/0x3f0
kernel: [519945.039677]    process_one_work+0x20f/0x410
kernel: [519945.039705]    worker_thread+0x34/0x400
kernel: [519945.039736]    kthread+0x120/0x140
kernel: [519945.039751]    ? process_one_work+0x410/0x410
kernel: [519945.039764]    ? __kthread_parkme+0x70/0x70
kernel: [519945.039789]    ret_from_fork+0x35/0x40
kernel: [519945.039849] MY post_handler: p-
>addr=0x000000001ecd1ebc, eflags=0x246
```

Linux crash tool

Linux crash tool is another tool which helps in analyzing the kernel on goings. It can also be used to debug a generated kernel crash. It can also be used for live kernel debugging.

Let's write a kernel module to generate a deadlock and try to debug it using live kernel analysis.

We have written a simple kernel module to generate a deadlock :

Program to create a deadlock

```
#include<linux/module.h>
#include<linux/version.h>
#include<linux/kernel.h>
#include<linux/semaphore.h>

#include<linux/kthread.h>
#include<linux/sched.h>
#include<linux/delay.h>
#include<linux/slab.h>

struct semaphore sync1;
```

```
struct semaphore sync2;
struct task_struct *task1;
struct task_struct *task2;
int shared_var;
int data;

int thread_function_one(void *data)
{
    int ret = 10;
    int cpu1;
    printk(KERN_INFO "IN THREAD FUNCTION 1 \n");

    while(!kthread_should_stop()){
        down(&sync1);
        cpu1 = get_cpu();
        put_cpu();
        printk("t1 cpu = %d shared_var =
%d\n",cpu1,shared_var);
        msleep(1000);
        down(&sync2);
        up(&sync2);
        up(&sync1);
    }
    printk(KERN_INFO "EXIT from thread function 1\n");
    return ret;
}

int thread_function_two(void *data)
{
    int ret = 10;
    int cpu2;
    printk(KERN_INFO "IN THREAD FUNCTION 2 \n");

    while(!kthread_should_stop()){
        down(&sync2);
        cpu2 = get_cpu();
        put_cpu();
```

```
        printk("t2 cpu = %d shared_var =
%d\n",cpu2,shared_var);
        msleep(2000);
        down(&sync1);
        up(&sync1);
        up(&sync2);
    }
    printk(KERN_INFO "EXIT from thread function 2\n");
    return ret;
}

static int kernel_init(void)
{
    int cpu3;
    sema_init(&sync1, 1);
    sema_init(&sync2, 1);
    printk(KERN_INFO "module_init address of sync1 = %p
sync2 = %p\n",&sync1, &sync2);

    cpu3 = get_cpu();
    put_cpu();
    printk("main thread cpu = %d \n",cpu3);

    shared_var = 0;
    task1 = kthread_create(&thread_function_one,(void
*)&data,"one");
    kthread_bind(task1, cpu3);
    wake_up_process(task1);

    cpu3 = 3;
    task2 = kthread_create(&thread_function_two,(void
*)&data,"two");
    kthread_bind(task2, cpu3);
    wake_up_process(task2);

    return 0;
}
```

```
static void kernel_exit(void)
{
    kthread_stop(task1);
    kthread_stop(task2);
    printk(KERN_INFO "module_exit\n");
}


module_init(kernel_init);
module_exit(kernel_exit);

MODULE_AUTHOR("K_K");
MODULE_DESCRIPTION("SIMPLE MODULE");
MODULE_LICENSE("GPL");
```

Here we launch 2 kernel threads and try to take the 2 semaphores:

In thread "one" the semaphores are acquired in the order sync1 --> sync2.
Also they are released in the order sync2 --> sync1

```
        down(&sync1);
        cpu1 = get_cpu();
    ...
    ...
        down(&sync2);
        up(&sync2);
        up(&sync1);
```

In thread "two" we acquire the semaphores in reverse order sync2 --> sync1.
Also they are released in the order sync1 --> sync2

```
    down(&sync2);
        cpu2 = get_cpu();
    ...
    ...
        down(&sync1);
        up(&sync1);
        up(&sync2);
```

If we launch this program, we see that these 2 threads get entangled in a deadlock. This is a classic case of ABBA deadlock.
(The solution for this is correct lock ordering)

The print from the "dmesg" shows following :

```
Feb 17 20:36:45 x-vm kernel: [ 5698.602062] example:
loading out-of-tree module taints kernel.
Feb 17 20:36:45 x-vm kernel: [ 5698.602204] example: module
verification failed: signature and/or required key missing
- tainting kernel
Feb 17 20:36:45 x-vm kernel: [ 5698.620436] module_init
address of sync1 = 000000004182d7f4 sync2 =
000000008c26dfea
Feb 17 20:36:45 x-vm kernel: [ 5698.620440] main thread cpu
= 5
Feb 17 20:36:45 x-vm kernel: [ 5698.620595] IN THREAD
FUNCTION 1
Feb 17 20:36:45 x-vm kernel: [ 5698.620600] t1 cpu = 5
shared_var = 0
Feb 17 20:36:45 x-vm kernel: [ 5698.622273] IN THREAD
FUNCTION 2
Feb 17 20:36:45 x-vm kernel: [ 5698.622279] t2 cpu = 3
shared_var = 0
```

The "ps" command shows 2 kernel thread in UNINTERRUPTIBLE SLEEP (indicated by the thread state "D") :
ps :
```
1 D root      7105     2  0  80   0  -     0 down   20:36 ?
00:00:00 [one]
1 D root      7106     2  0  80   0  -     0 down   20:36 ?
00:00:00 [two]
```

We can get the backtrace of these threads using the following command :
```
echo t > /proc/sysrq-trigger
```

It generates a lot of output in kernel logs. It dumps the stack of all the kernel processes in kernel logs.

For our 2 threads we get the following call stack :

Call stack for thread one :

```
Feb 17 20:38:57 x-vm kernel: [ 5829.968986] one              D    0
7105      2 0x80000000
Feb 17 20:38:57 x-vm kernel: [ 5829.968992] Call Trace:
Feb 17 20:38:57 x-vm kernel: [ 5829.969004]  __schedule+0x2d0/0x840
Feb 17 20:38:57 x-vm kernel: [ 5829.969013]  ? schedule+0x5/0x70
Feb 17 20:38:57 x-vm kernel: [ 5829.969032]  schedule+0x2c/0x70
Feb 17 20:38:57 x-vm kernel: [ 5829.969039]
schedule_timeout+0x258/0x360
Feb 17 20:38:57 x-vm kernel: [ 5829.969049]  ?
schedule_timeout+0x5/0x360
Feb 17 20:38:57 x-vm kernel: [ 5829.969064]  __down+0x86/0xd0
Feb 17 20:38:57 x-vm kernel: [ 5829.969073]  ? down_trylock+0x30/0x40
Feb 17 20:38:57 x-vm kernel: [ 5829.969085]  down+0x41/0x50
Feb 17 20:38:57 x-vm kernel: [ 5829.969097]
thread_function_one+0x71/0x90 [example]
Feb 17 20:38:57 x-vm kernel: [ 5829.969105]  kthread+0x120/0x140
Feb 17 20:38:57 x-vm kernel: [ 5829.969112]  ? 0xffffffffc0584000
Feb 17 20:38:57 x-vm kernel: [ 5829.969117]  ?
__kthread_parkme+0x70/0x70
Feb 17 20:38:57 x-vm kernel: [ 5829.969128]  ret_from_fork+0x35/0x40
```

Call stack for thread two :

```
Feb 17 20:38:57 x-vm kernel: [ 5829.969154] two              D    0
7106      2 0x80000000
Feb 17 20:38:57 x-vm kernel: [ 5829.969160] Call Trace:
Feb 17 20:38:57 x-vm kernel: [ 5829.969173]  __schedule+0x2d0/0x840
Feb 17 20:38:57 x-vm kernel: [ 5829.969182]  ? schedule+0x5/0x70
Feb 17 20:38:57 x-vm kernel: [ 5829.969196]  schedule+0x2c/0x70
Feb 17 20:38:57 x-vm kernel: [ 5829.969202]
schedule_timeout+0x258/0x360
Feb 17 20:38:57 x-vm kernel: [ 5829.969212]  ?
schedule_timeout+0x5/0x360
Feb 17 20:38:57 x-vm kernel: [ 5829.969227]  __down+0x86/0xd0
Feb 17 20:38:57 x-vm kernel: [ 5829.969236]  ? down_trylock+0x30/0x40
Feb 17 20:38:57 x-vm kernel: [ 5829.969247]  down+0x41/0x50
```

```
Feb 17 20:38:57 x-vm kernel: [ 5829.969257]
thread_function_two+0x71/0x90 [example]
Feb 17 20:38:57 x-vm kernel: [ 5829.969265]  kthread+0x120/0x140
Feb 17 20:38:57 x-vm kernel: [ 5829.969272]  ?
thread_function_one+0x90/0x90 [example]
Feb 17 20:38:57 x-vm kernel: [ 5829.969277]  ?
__kthread_parkme+0x70/0x70
Feb 17 20:38:57 x-vm kernel: [ 5829.969288]  ret_from_fork+0x35/0x40
```

We see that they are both waiting at "__down()" which is the function for acquiring the semaphore.

We can use the Linux crash tool to view the same. The Linux crash tool has the advantage of enabling us to read the values of stack variables.

If we want to debug a core generated because of kernel crash we need to give the same command with core generated.
```
# crash /usr/lib/debug/lib/modules/3.15.X.XX-
XXX.XX.X.el7.x86_64/vmlinux /path/to/vmcore
```

A live system can be debugged using the crash utility. Following is the command for same :
```
# crash /usr/lib/debug/lib/modules/3.15.X.XX-
XXX.XX.X.el7.x86_64/vmlinux
```

The above command will give a prompt to start the live debugging of the kernel.

1. ps command : We can see the current threads run by the linux kernel using the crash ps command. This is similar to the shell ps command but gives the "task_struct" address for the running threads.

2. set command : We can then set the context of any thread to the "task_struct" address of the thread using the "set" command.
```
crash> set ffff88007b1aa220
    PID: 3580
COMMAND: "one"
```

```
    TASK: ffff88007b1aa220  [THREAD_INFO: ffff880079572000]
     CPU: 1
   STATE: TASK_UNINTERRUPTIBLE

crash> set ffff88007b1ac440
     PID: 3581
COMMAND: "two"
    TASK: ffff88007b1ac440  [THREAD_INFO: ffff880034834000]
     CPU: 3
   STATE: TASK_UNINTERRUPTIBLE
```

3. bt command : To get the thread stack of a context we can use the "bt" command. bt stands for backtrace.

```
crash> bt
PID: 3580   TASK: ffff88007b1aa220  CPU: 1   COMMAND: "one"
 #0 [ffff880079573cf0] __schedule at ffffffff815f14fd
 #1 [ffff880079573d58] schedule at ffffffff815f1a39
 #2 [ffff880079573d68] schedule_timeout at ffffffff815ef939
 #3 [ffff880079573e10] __down_common at ffffffff815f0f32
 #4 [ffff880079573e88] __down at ffffffff815f0fc7
 #5 [ffff880079573e98] down at ffffffff8108b8c1
 #6 [ffff880079573eb8] thread_function_one at
ffffffffa0534073 [threads]
 #7 [ffff880079573ec8] kthread at ffffffff81085b0f
 #8 [ffff880079573f50] ret_from_fork at ffffffff815fc8ec
crash> bt
PID: 3581   TASK: ffff88007b1ac440  CPU: 3   COMMAND: "two"
 #0 [ffff880034835cf0] __schedule at ffffffff815f14fd
 #1 [ffff880034835d58] schedule at ffffffff815f1a39
 #2 [ffff880034835d68] schedule_timeout at ffffffff815ef939
 #3 [ffff880034835e10] __down_common at ffffffff815f0f32
 #4 [ffff880034835e88] __down at ffffffff815f0fc7
 #5 [ffff880034835e98] down at ffffffff8108b8c1
 #6 [ffff880034835eb8] thread_function_two at
ffffffffa0534103 [threads]
 #7 [ffff880034835ec8] kthread at ffffffff81085b0f
 #8 [ffff880034835f50] ret_from_fork at ffffffff815fc8ec
```

4. bt -f : We might need to get the values of local variables in the current context. The addresses of the variables can be fetched using the "bt -f" command.

Let's see the output of this for our hung thread:

```
crash> bt -f
PID: 3581   TASK: ffff88007b1ac440  CPU: 3   COMMAND: "two"
 #0 [ffff880034835cf0] __schedule at ffffffff815f14fd
    ffff880034835cf8: 0000000000000046 ffff880034835fd8
    ffff880034835d08: 0000000000014580 ffff880034835fd8
    ffff880034835d18: 0000000000014580 ffff88007b1ac440
    ffff880034835d28: ffffffffa0536280 7fffffffffffffff
    ffff880034835d38: ffff88007b1ac440 0000000000000002
    ffff880034835d48: 0000000000000000 ffff880034835d60
    ffff880034835d58: ffffffff815f1a39
 #1 [ffff880034835d58] schedule at ffffffff815f1a39
    ffff880034835d60: ffff880034835e08 ffffffff815ef939
 #2 [ffff880034835d68] schedule_timeout at ffffffff815ef939
    ffff880034835d70: 7fffffffffffffff ffff880034835da8
    ffff880034835d80: ffffffff8106e37b ffff880034835e10
    ffff880034835d90: ffff88007c514000 0000000000000286
    ffff880034835da0: 0000000000000000 ffff880034835dd8
    ffff880034835db0: ffffffff8106f06e 0000000000000286
    ffff880034835dc0: 000000001daef83c ffff880034835e10
    ffff880034835dd0: ffff880034835e10 000000001daef83c
    ffff880034835de0: ffffffffa0536280 7fffffffffffffff
    ffff880034835df0: ffff88007b1ac440 0000000000000002
    ffff880034835e00: 0000000000000000 ffff880034835e80
    ffff880034835e10: ffffffff815f0f32
 #3 [ffff880034835e10] __down_common at ffffffff815f0f32
    ffff880034835e18: 0000000000000000 ffffffffa0536288
    ffff880034835e28: ffffffffa0536288 ffff88007b1ac440
    ffff880034835e38: ffff88007b1ac400 ffffffffffffffff
    ffff880034835e48: 000000001daef83c 0000000000000000
    ffff880034835e58: ffffffffa0536280 ffffffffa0536240
    ffff880034835e68: ffffffffa0534090 0000000000000000
    ffff880034835e78: 0000000000000000 ffff880034835e90
```

```
     ffff880034835e88: ffffffff815f0fc7
 #4 [ffff880034835e88] __down at ffffffff815f0fc7
     ffff880034835e90: ffff880034835eb0 ffffffff8108b8c1
 #5 [ffff880034835e98] down at ffffffff8108b8c1
     ffff880034835ea0: 0000000000000286 ffff880079ac7cb8
     ffff880034835eb0: ffff880034835ec0 ffffffffa0534103
 #6 [ffff880034835eb8] thread_function_two at
ffffffffa0534103 [threads]
     ffff880034835ec0: ffff880034835f48 ffffffff81085b0f
 #7 [ffff880034835ec8] kthread at ffffffff81085b0f
     ffff880034835ed0: 0000000000000000 0000000000000000
     ffff880034835ee0: ffffffffa0536240 0000000000000000
     ffff880034835ef0: 0000000000000000 ffff880034835ef8
     ffff880034835f00: ffff880034835ef8 ffff880000000000
     ffff880034835f10: ffff880000000000 ffff880034835f18
     ffff880034835f20: ffff880034835f18 000000001daef83c
     ffff880034835f30: ffffffff81085a40 0000000000000000
     ffff880034835f40: 0000000000000000 ffff880079ac7cb8
     ffff880034835f50: ffffffff815fc8ec
 #8 [ffff880034835f50] ret_from_fork at ffffffff815fc8ec
```

Here the addresses are pointing to the local variables. There are a hell of a lot of addresses here, which makes it difficult to trace our variable. Generally because of optimizations these variables appear at different places in the stack.

What one can do is, at the start of the module print the addresses of these variables : ;

```
Dec 12 02:49:25 localhost kernel: module_init address of
sync1 = ffffffffa0536280 sync2 = ffffffffa0536260
```

5. Fetching the values of the variables :
Once the variable address is known to us we can just give commands in the following fashion, to fetch the values of the variable.

```
crash> struct semaphore ffffffffa0536280
struct semaphore {
  lock = {
```

```
      raw_lock = {
        {
          head_tail = 262148,
          tickets = {
            head = 4,
            tail = 4
          }
        }
      }
    },
    count = 0,
    wait_list = {
      next = 0xffff880034835e20,
      prev = 0xffff880034835e20
    }
  }

crash> struct semaphore ffffffffa0536260
struct semaphore {
  lock = {
    raw_lock = {
      {
        head_tail = 262148,
        tickets = {
          head = 4,
          tail = 4
        }
      }
    }
  },
  count = 0,
  wait_list = {
    next = 0xffff880079573e20,
    prev = 0xffff880079573e20
  }
}
```

Chapter 3 Linux process insights

Linux process Address space

We will start this chapter with the layout of a normal C program. The stages by which a C program(text) becomes a process includes compilation and loading the compiled file, the executable.

Once the executable is loaded, it becomes a process. In Linux an executable file is in ELF format, executable linkable format.

This ELF format has ".data" and ".text" sections present. The ".data" section has the place for global, static data variables. ".text" has the code of the C program in machine language.

When this ELF format executable is loaded, a program comes into existence. At the time of loading the sections of the ELF file becomes the sections in the process address space of the process.

What does this look like :

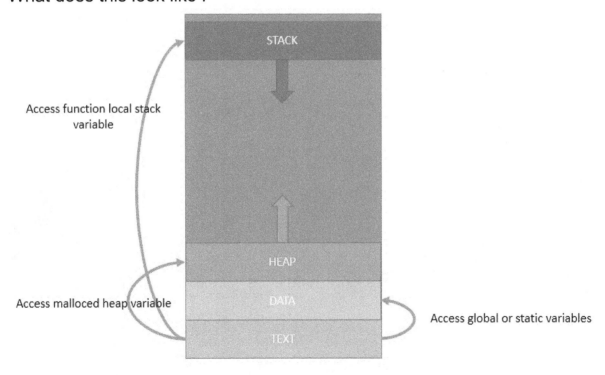

Let's write a C program which accesses data stored in all the sections possible:

```
#include <stdio.h>
#include <stdlib.h>

static unsigned int static_var = 1000;
unsigned int global_var = 1000;

int main()
{
        unsigned int stack_var = 1000;
        unsigned int *heap_var = NULL;
        heap_var = (unsigned int *)malloc(sizeof(unsigned
int));
        *heap_var = 1000;

        static_var++;
        global_var++;
        stack_var++;
        (*heap_var)++;

        printf("static = %d, global = %d, stack = %d, heap
= %d\n", static_var, global_var, stack_var, *heap_var);
        printf("static addr = %p, global addr = %p, stack
addr = %p, heap addr =  %p text addr = %p\n", &static_var,
&global_var, &stack_var, heap_var, &main);

        while(1)
        {
                sleep(1);
        }

        return;
}
```

We compile it using gcc :
```
# gcc -g program.c -o program
```

Let's use objdump utility to see the sections of data and text.

```
# objdump -s program
...
Contents of section .text:
 4004d0 31ed4989 d15e4889 e24883e4 f0505449
1.I..^H..H...PTI
 4004e0 c7c00007 400048c7 c1900640 0048c7c7
....@.H....@.H..
...
Contents of section .rodata:
 400710 01000200 00000000 00000000 00000000
................
 400720 73746174 6963203d 2025642c 20676c6f    static = %d,
glo
 400730 62616c20 3d202564 2c207374 61636b20    bal = %d,
stack
 400740 3d202564 2c206865 6170203d 2025640a    = %d, heap =
%d
...
Contents of section .data:
 601040 00000000 e8030000 e8030000              ............
...
```

We can see that the "rodata" section has the string literals.
Let's see the disassembly of the program using "objdump -S".

```
# objdump -S program

00000000004005bd <main>:

static unsigned int static_var = 1000;
unsigned int global_var = 1000;

int main()
{
  4005bd:       55                              push   %rbp
  4005be:       48 89 e5                        mov    %rsp,%rbp
```

```
 4005c1:         48 83 ec 10              sub     $0x10,%rsp
        unsigned int stack_var = 1000;
 4005c5:         c7 45 f4 e8 03 00 00     movl    $0x3e8,-
0xc(%rbp)
        unsigned int *heap_var = NULL;
 4005cc:         48 c7 45 f8 00 00 00     movq    $0x0,-
0x8(%rbp)
 4005d3:         00
        heap_var = (unsigned int *)malloc(sizeof(unsigned
int));
 4005d4:         bf 04 00 00 00           mov     $0x4,%edi
 4005d9:         e8 d2 fe ff ff           callq   4004b0
<malloc@plt>
 4005de:         48 89 45 f8              mov     %rax,-
0x8(%rbp)
        *heap_var = 1000;
 4005e2:         48 8b 45 f8              mov     -
0x8(%rbp),%rax
 4005e6:         c7 00 e8 03 00 00        movl
$0x3e8,(%rax)


        static_var++;
 4005ec:         8b 05 52 0a 20 00        mov
0x200a52(%rip),%eax        # 601044 <static_var>
 4005f2:         83 c0 01                 add     $0x1,%eax
 4005f5:         89 05 49 0a 20 00        mov
%eax,0x200a49(%rip)        # 601044 <static_var>
        global_var++;
 4005fb:         8b 05 47 0a 20 00        mov
0x200a47(%rip),%eax        # 601048 <global_var>
 400601:         83 c0 01                 add     $0x1,%eax
 400604:         89 05 3e 0a 20 00        mov
%eax,0x200a3e(%rip)        # 601048 <global_var>
        stack_var++;
 40060a:         8b 45 f4                 mov     -
0xc(%rbp),%eax
 40060d:         83 c0 01                 add     $0x1,%eax
```

```
    400610:         89 45 f4                    mov    %eax,-
0xc(%rbp)
        (*heap_var)++;
    400613:         48 8b 45 f8                 mov    -
0x8(%rbp),%rax
    400617:         8b 00                       mov    (%rax),%eax
    400619:         8d 50 01                    lea
0x1(%rax),%edx
    40061c:         48 8b 45 f8                 mov    -
0x8(%rbp),%rax
    400620:         89 10                       mov    %edx,(%rax)


        printf("static = %d, global = %d, stack = %d, heap
= %d\n", static_var, global_var, stack_var, *heap_var);
    400622:         48 8b 45 f8                 mov    -
0x8(%rbp),%rax
    400626:         8b 30                       mov    (%rax),%esi
    400628:         8b 4d f4                    mov    -
0xc(%rbp),%ecx
    40062b:         8b 15 17 0a 20 00           mov
0x200a17(%rip),%edx        # 601048 <global_var>
    400631:         8b 05 0d 0a 20 00           mov
0x200a0d(%rip),%eax        # 601044 <static_var>
    400637:         41 89 f0                    mov    %esi,%r8d
    40063a:         89 c6                       mov    %eax,%esi
    40063c:         bf 20 07 40 00              mov
$0x400720,%edi
    400641:         b8 00 00 00 00              mov    $0x0,%eax
    400646:         e8 35 fe ff ff              callq  400480
<printf@plt>
        printf("static addr = %p, global addr = %p, stack
addr = %p, heap addr =  %p text addr = %p\n", &static_var,
&global_var, &stack_var, heap_var, &main);
    40064b:         48 8b 55 f8                 mov    -
0x8(%rbp),%rdx
    40064f:         48 8d 45 f4                 lea    -
0xc(%rbp),%rax
```

```
   400653:           41 b9 bd 05 40 00          mov
$0x4005bd,%r9d
   400659:           49 89 d0                   mov     %rdx,%r8
   40065c:           48 89 c1                   mov     %rax,%rcx
   40065f:           ba 48 10 60 00             mov
$0x601048,%edx
   400664:           be 44 10 60 00             mov
$0x601044,%esi
   400669:           bf 58 07 40 00             mov
$0x400758,%edi
   40066e:           b8 00 00 00 00             mov     $0x0,%eax
   400673:           e8 08 fe ff ff             callq   400480
<printf@plt>
```

Let's see the output of this program to see the addresses of the variables for all of these static, global, heap and stack variables.

```
static = 1001, global = 1001, stack = 1001, heap = 1001
```
static addr = 0x601044, global addr = 0x601048, stack addr = 0x7ffd94344af4, heap addr = 0x161d010 text addr = 0x4005bd

We can see these addresses are actually part of the C program. The mapping of all the sections of any running program is present in "/proc/<PID>" maps.

Let's see the same for our C program.

```
# ps -eafl | grep a.out
0 S root      15911 15503  0  80   0 -  1075 hrtime 08:26
pts/1    00:00:00 ./a.out
[root@localhost ~]# cat /proc/15911/maps
00400000-00401000 r-xp 00000000 fd:00 71239507
/root/c_prog/a.out
00600000-00601000 r--p 00000000 fd:00 71239507
/root/c_prog/a.out
```

```
00601000-00602000 rw-p 00001000 fd:00 71239507
/root/c_prog/a.out
0161d000-0163e000 rw-p 00000000 00:00 0
[heap]
7f529e0e3000-7f529e29b000 r-xp 00000000 fd:00 33597987
/usr/lib64/libc-2.17.so
7f529e29b000-7f529e49b000 ---p 001b8000 fd:00 33597987
/usr/lib64/libc-2.17.so
7f529e49b000-7f529e49f000 r--p 001b8000 fd:00 33597987
/usr/lib64/libc-2.17.so
7f529e49f000-7f529e4a1000 rw-p 001bc000 fd:00 33597987
/usr/lib64/libc-2.17.so
7f529e4a1000-7f529e4a6000 rw-p 00000000 00:00 0
7f529e4a6000-7f529e4c7000 r-xp 00000000 fd:00 33597980
/usr/lib64/ld-2.17.so
7f529e6ac000-7f529e6af000 rw-p 00000000 00:00 0
7f529e6c5000-7f529e6c7000 rw-p 00000000 00:00 0
7f529e6c7000-7f529e6c8000 r--p 00021000 fd:00 33597980
/usr/lib64/ld-2.17.so
7f529e6c8000-7f529e6c9000 rw-p 00022000 fd:00 33597980
/usr/lib64/ld-2.17.so
7f529e6c9000-7f529e6ca000 rw-p 00000000 00:00 0
7ffd94325000-7ffd94346000 rw-p 00000000 00:00 0
[stack]
7ffd9434a000-7ffd9434c000 r-xp 00000000 00:00 0
[vdso]
ffffffffff600000-ffffffffff601000 r-xp 00000000 00:00 0
[vsyscall]
```

We can see that the address range "00400000-00401000 r-xp" has permissions read and execute.

We can also see that the "&main" address belongs to this address range. This address range belongs to the ".text" region.

Similarly, the stack variable address "0x7ffd94344af4" belongs to the following address range :

```
7ffd94325000-7ffd94346000 rw-p 00000000 00:00 0
[stack]
```
Check out the permissions, it is read and write.

Static and global variables addresses belong to the data section with following addresses.
```
static addr = 0x601044, global addr = 0x601048,
00601000-00602000 rw-p 00001000 fd:00 71239507
/root/c_prog/a.out
```

A malloced variable from heap has the following address :
```
heap addr =  0x161d010
This variable belongs to the heap section :
0161d000-0163e000 rw-p 00000000 00:00 0
[heap]
```

All these sections combined are called "process address space" as a process can access these many addresses. The address space is composed of all these sections.

User space and kernel space

Every process in Linux has a userspace part and a kernel space footprint. The control of a process moves from userspace to kernel space when needed. Generally, the control moves when a user space process calls a system call.

The user space part of a program has a stack where a function runs its own heap, data section etc. When the control moves to the kernel, say after a system call, the kernel code, data and stack starts getting used.

We can see where the kernel code data heap and stack segments reside.

kernel code segment is a "_text" section. Its value can be fetched using :

```
root@x-vm:~# cat /proc/kallsyms | grep _text
ffffffffa0200000 T _text
```

kernel code segment end is "_etext".

```
root@x-vm:~# cat /proc/kallsyms | grep _etext
ffffffffa1000e81 T _etext
```

Similarly, kernel data segment start and end can also be fetched.

```
root@x-vm:~# cat /proc/kallsyms | grep _edata
ffffffffa1a52f40 D _edata
root@x-vm:~# cat /proc/kallsyms | grep _sdata
ffffffffa1800000 D _sdata
```

We can see the address of any Linux function using the "/proc/kallsyms" interface.

If we see properly we notice that the kernel virtual addresses range from 0xFFFFFFFF80000000 to 0xFFFFFFFFFFFFFFFF and user space virtual addresses start from 0x0000000000000000 to 0x00007FFFFFFFFFFF

These address ranges are not there just by chance. Actually, there is a division between the kernel space addresses and the user space virtual addresses. If we take a 64-bit processor which can access 2^{64} addresses, then the user space addresses are from 0 to 2^{48} and upper 2^{48} addresses are reserved for the kernel space.

The following diagram shows the organisation and division of virtual memory between kernel and user space.

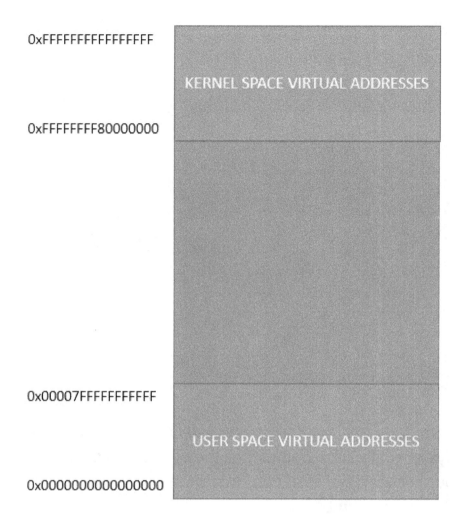

OxFFFFFFFFFFFFFFFF

KERNEL SPACE VIRTUAL ADDRESSES

OxFFFFFFFF80000000

Ox00007FFFFFFFFFFF

USER SPACE VIRTUAL ADDRESSES

Ox0000000000000000

System calls

System calls are a way in which user space programs can call the kernel of the operating system. System calls can be used for process creation, memory allocation, file access, networking etc.

The x86 system provides rings of privileges. The ring with the maximum number has the least privileges, whereas the ring with the minimum number has the most privileges. In a system which supports 4 rings, ring 3 is the ring where the applications run. They can execute only a part of the processor instruction set. Ring 0, where the kernel runs has the highest privileges and can run processor instructions. System calls are a way through which control moves from ring 3 to ring 0.

The following figure shows the execution of a system call.

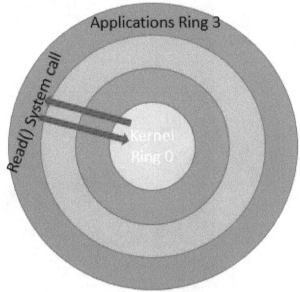

All the system calls are statically compiled in the Linux kernel. The total number of system calls is predefined. All the system calls have an associated index number present. For example, "read()" system call has index number 0, "fork()" has index number 35. When a system call is called the index number of the system call is passed, also the control is passed to the kernel. To handle the system call the kernel fetches the system call index number and uses it to find the matching system call handler in the "system_call_table".

The x86_64 user programs invoke a system call by putting the system call number (0 for "read()") into the RAX register, and the other parameters into specific registers (RDI, RSI, RDX for the first 3 parameters), then issue the x86_64 "SYSCALL" instruction.

This instruction causes the processor to transition to ring 0 and invoke the function referenced by the "MSR_LSTAR" model-specific register.

The first kernel function which gets called for every system call is defined in entry_64.S kernel file. The location of this file is arch/x86/entry/entry_64.S

For 64-bit systems we can see the first function called is entry_SYSCALL_64_after_hwframe. This function is defined in this entry_64.S file.

We can see that entry_SYSCALL_64_after_hwframe calls do_syscall_64.

```
ENTRY(system_call)
...
 call     do_syscall_64        /* returns with IRQs disabled */
...
END(system_call)
```

We can see the implementation of "do_syscall_64()" in "arch/x86/entry/common.c".

```
__visible void do_syscall_64(unsigned long nr, struct
pt_regs *regs)
{
.
        regs->ax = sys_call_table[nr](regs);
.
}
```

We can clearly see that "sys_call_table" is indexed based on the index number of the system call.

We also see that any "dump_stack" in any kernel function gives the same call sequence mentioned in this chapter. For example if we put a kprobe on "_do_fork()" function and "dump_stack()" in entry of this function, then we get following call stack:

```
kernel: [85812.999073]  dump_stack+0x63/0x8a
kernel: [85812.999083]  handler_pre+0x2c/0x30
[kprobe_example]
kernel: [85812.999087]  kprobe_ftrace_handler+0x8f/0xf0
kernel: [85812.999090]  ftrace_ops_assist_func+0x87/0xf0
```

```
kernel: [85812.999094]  0xffffffffc080b0d5
kernel: [85812.999105]  _do_fork+0x5/0x3a0
kernel: [85812.999108]   __x64_sys_clone+0x27/0x30
kernel: [85812.999119]  do_syscall_64+0x5a/0x110
kernel: [85812.999124]
entry_SYSCALL_64_after_hwframe+0x44/0xa9
kernel: [85812.999127] RIP: 0033:0x7f446c4a0881
```

Let us have some fun and write a userspace program to call a system call using its number. In this C program we call the chmod system call using the syscall interface. System call number for a particular system call can be fetched from this header file:
```
/usr/include/x86_64-linux-gnu/asm/unistd_64.h
```

We can see the contents of this file :
```
#define __NR_read 0
#define __NR_write 1
#define __NR_open 2
#define __NR_close 3
...
#define __NR_chmod 90
...
```

```c
#include <stdio.h>
#include <unistd.h>
#include <sys/syscall.h>
#include <errno.h>
int main()
{
    int ret;
    ret = syscall(90, "/root/c_prog/syscall.c", 0444);
    if (rc == -1)
        printf("chmod failed, errno = %d\n", errno);
    return 0;
}
```

This program changes the permission of "syscall.c" file to 0444.

Linux process descriptor

Every process's kernel footprint consists of a number of data structures.
These data structures have details and functionality related to the process.
To illustrate a few :
1. The process PID.
2. The code, data, stack heap sections.
3. Kernel stack of a process.
4. Scheduler information.
5. Signal queue and signal handler's information.
6. Process's page tables.

The first and most important data structure is the "struct task_struct".
It is composed of many important data structures. All the sections of code, data, stack, heap, etc. are linked to "task_struct" using "mm_struct". These sections are called Virtual memory areas or VMAs or VAs.

task_struct -> mm_struct -> vm_area_struct (points to the sections for code, data, stack, heap, etc.)

Kernel stack of the process is contained in "*stack"
task_struct -> stack

The process page tables are present in the "pgd" field of the memory descriptor.
task_struct -> mm_struct -> pgd

The signals and the signal handler information are present in signal related structures.
task_struct -> signal

task_struct -> sighand

Lets try to print the sections start and end addresses of the VMAs from the kernel. This program prints the start and end addresses of VMAs.

```c
/**
 * app.c
 *
 * @brief User program to trigger own module
 *
 *
 */
#include <stdio.h>
#include <stdlib.h>
#include <string.h>
#include <sys/stat.h>
#include <fcntl.h>
#include <sys/ioctl.h>
#include <unistd.h>
#include <error.h>
#include <sys/types.h>

#define MY_MAGIC 'H'
#define IOCTL_DISPLAY_TS _IOR(MY_MAGIC, 0, int)

int main()
{
    int fd = -1, ret;
    int ret_val = 0;
    fd = open("/dev/my_char_device", O_RDWR);
    ret_val = ioctl(fd, IOCTL_DISPLAY_TS, NULL);
    getchar();
    close(fd);
    return 0;
}
```

The kernel space driver module :

```
#include <linux/kernel.h>
#include <linux/module.h>
#include <linux/init.h>
#include <linux/types.h>
#include <linux/major.h>
#include <linux/kdev_t.h>
#include <linux/fs.h>
#include <linux/device.h>
#include <linux/cdev.h>
#include <linux/slab.h>
#include <linux/stat.h>
#include <asm/uaccess.h>
#include <linux/sched/signal.h>

dev_t my_devt;
char mydrv_name[] = "my_char_device";
struct class *my_class;
struct device *my_char_dev;
struct cdev my_cdev;

ssize_t my_read(struct file *my_file, char __user *my_buf,
size_t len, loff_t *loff);
ssize_t my_write(struct file *my_file, const char __user
*my_buf, size_t len, loff_t *loff);
long my_ioctl(struct file *, unsigned int, unsigned long);

struct file_operations myfops =  {
    .owner = THIS_MODULE,
    .read  = my_read,
    .write = my_write,
    .unlocked_ioctl = my_ioctl,
};

#define MY_MAGIC 'H'
#define IOCTL_DISPLAY_TS _IOR(MY_MAGIC, 0, int)
```

```c
int create_char_device(void)
{
    int ret = 0;

    printk(KERN_INFO "create_char_device: I'm
executing....\n");

    if( 0 > (ret = alloc_chrdev_region(&my_devt, 0, 1,
mydrv_name)))
    {
        printk(KERN_ERR "create_char_device:
alloc_chrdev_region failed\n");
    }

    printk(KERN_INFO "dev_t major is {%d} and minor is {%d}
\n", MAJOR(my_devt), MINOR(my_devt));
    if( NULL == (my_class = class_create(THIS_MODULE,
"my_class_name")))
    {
        printk(KERN_ERR "class_create failed...!\n");
    }
    printk(KERN_INFO "Class created with name {%s}\n",
my_class->name);

    if(NULL == (my_char_dev = device_create(my_class, NULL,
my_devt, NULL, mydrv_name)))
    {
        printk(KERN_ERR "device_create failed...!\n");
    }

    cdev_init(&my_cdev, &myfops);
    cdev_add(&my_cdev, my_devt, 1);

    return 0;
}
```

```
ssize_t my_read(struct file *my_file, char __user *my_buf,
size_t len, loff_t *loff)
{
    return 0;
}

ssize_t my_write(struct file *my_file, const  char  __user
*my_buf, size_t len, loff_t *loff)
{
    return 0;
}

void display_vma(void)
{
    struct task_struct *task = current;

    printk(KERN_INFO "************************Start PS -
EF******************");

    for_each_process(task) {
        printk("For the process %s[%d] \n", task->comm,
task->pid);

        if( (NULL != task->mm) && (NULL != task->mm->mmap)
)
        {
            struct vm_area_struct *next = NULL;

            next = task->mm->mmap;
            do {
                printk("\t vm_start:0x%lx  vm_end:0x%lx
\n",
                        next->vm_start, next->vm_end);
                next = next->vm_next;
            } while(NULL != next);
        }
```

```c
        if( (NULL != task->active_mm) && (NULL != task->active_mm->mmap) )
        {
                struct vm_area_struct *next = NULL;

                printk("***USing Active_mm**************\n");
                next = task->active_mm->mmap;
                do {
                    printk(" vm_start:0x%lx  vm_end:0x%lx \n",
                            next->vm_start, next->vm_end);
                    next = next->vm_next;
                } while(NULL != next);
        }
    }
    return 1;
}



long  my_ioctl(struct file *file, unsigned int ioctl_num,
unsigned long ioctl_param )
{
    char *temp;
    char ch;
    int i;

    switch(ioctl_num)
    {
        case IOCTL_DISPLAY_TS:
            printk(KERN_ERR "in ioctl DISPLAY_TS");
            display_vma();
            break;
        default:
            printk(KERN_ERR "Default case executing-No
proper input case");
    }

    return 0;
}
```

```
int delete_char_device( void )
{
    cdev_del(&my_cdev);
    if(my_char_dev != NULL )
    {
        device_destroy(my_class, my_devt);
    }
    if(my_class != NULL )
    {
        class_destroy(my_class);
    }
    if(my_devt != 0)
    {
        unregister_chrdev_region(my_devt,1);
    }
    return 0;
}

static int __init my_init(void)
{
    printk("In my_init Kernel function\n");
    if( create_char_device())
    {
        printk(KERN_ERR "FAILED to create char device\n");
    }
    return 0;
}


static void __exit my_exit(void)
{
    printk("In MyExit/Cleanup Kernel function\n");

    if(delete_char_device())
    {
        printk(KERN_ERR "FAILED to delete char device\n");
```

```
    }
}

module_init(my_init);
module_exit(my_exit);

/** Description about module*/
MODULE_AUTHOR("Test");
MODULE_LICENSE("GPL");
```

The output of this program prints the addresses of all the VMAs for each process in the system:

```
kernel: [ 1103.925906] For the process sshd[2353]
kernel: [ 1103.925909]  vm_start:0x5628ffba4000
vm_end:0x5628ffc61000
kernel: [ 1103.925911]  vm_start:0x5628ffe60000
vm_end:0x5628ffe63000
kernel: [ 1103.925914]  vm_start:0x5628ffe63000
vm_end:0x5628ffe64000
kernel: [ 1103.925917]  vm_start:0x5628ffe64000
vm_end:0x5628ffe6d000
kernel: [ 1103.925919]  vm_start:0x562900596000
vm_end:0x5629005c6000
kernel: [ 1103.925922]  vm_start:0x5629005c6000
vm_end:0x5629005e7000
kernel: [ 1103.925925]  vm_start:0x7f5ab5096000
vm_end:0x7f5ab50d2000
kernel: [ 1103.925927]  vm_start:0x7f5ab50d2000
vm_end:0x7f5ab52d1000
kernel: [ 1103.925930]  vm_start:0x7f5ab52d1000
vm_end:0x7f5ab52d4000
kernel: [ 1103.925933]  vm_start:0x7f5ab52d4000
vm_end:0x7f5ab52d5000
```

Linux process creation

When a new process is created then a new set of resources need to be formed/allocated. These include formation of "task_struct", "mm_struct", "vm_area_struct", "pgd", "stack", etc.

"fork()", "vfork()" and "clone()" etc. are the system calls which create a process in Linux. When these system calls are invoked corresponding kernel space implementation is invoked.

If we see the implementation of "fork()" system call in the kernel, we see that it calls the kernel's "_do_fork()" function.

```
SYSCALL_DEFINE0(fork)
{
#ifdef CONFIG_MMU
        return _do_fork(SIGCHLD, 0, 0, NULL, NULL, 0);
#else
        /* can not support in nommu mode */
        return -EINVAL;
#endif
}
```

If we see the implementation of "vfork()" and "clone()", we again see that they call the same "do_fork()" function of kernel.

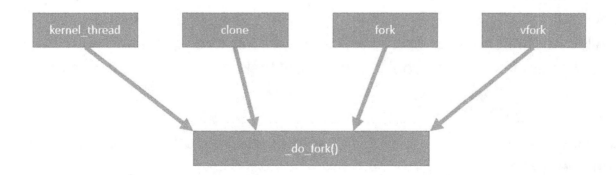

We can see that all the different system calls for "creation of processes" in Linux are implemented using the "_do_fork()" function call in the kernel. Now let's see the "do_fork()" implementation.

"do_fork()" function is called with different flags as per the caller's usage

"do_fork()" function calls "copy_process()" to do the major work.

```
do_fork --> copy_process
    -->dup_task_struct
    -->copy_creds
    -->sched_fork
```

The following calls (called by "copy_process()" only) are used to copy the process information :

```
    -->copy_semundo
    -->copy_files
    -->copy_fs
    -->copy_sighand
    -->copy_signal
    -->copy_mm
    -->copy_namespaces
    -->copy_io
    -->copy_thread
```

Now let's see the major functionality achieved in these calls :
"dup_task_struct" :
1. Allocates "task_struct" from "kmem_cache" : task_struct_cachep
2. Allocates "thread_info" from "kmem_cache" : thread_info_cache
3. "arch_dup_task_struct" copies the "parent task_struct" exactly to this child.

"sched_fork()" :
1. Initialises the "sched_entity" for a process. Includes initialization of vruntime, exec_start.
2. Makes the task state as TASK_NEW, so that nobody runs the process, or it's not kept in the run queue. The process will be put into running state later.

3. Initializes priority of task, taking care of the nice values.

4. Initializes scheduler class of the process to real time, fair scheduling.

"copy_files()" :

1. Copy file descriptor table "fdtable"

"copy_sighand()" :

1. copies the signal handlers of the parent process

"copy_signal()" :

1. Initialises more signal handler values

"copy_mm()" :

1. create a copy of the page tables. It does not copy the actual contents of the pages. Pages are newly allocated when a write comes to a page. (COW - Copy on write)

It calls "dup_mm()" :

```
--> Allocates mm_struct
--> Calls mm_init
--> Allocates pgd_alloc to allocate the page table
```

It calls pgd_ctor to copy the pgd entries from kernel :

```
if (PAGETABLE_LEVELS == 2 ||
  (PAGETABLE_LEVELS == 3 && SHARED_KERNEL_PMD) ||
  PAGETABLE_LEVELS == 4) {
  clone_pgd_range(pgd + KERNEL_PGD_BOUNDARY,
    swapper_pg_dir + KERNEL_PGD_BOUNDARY,
    KERNEL_PGD_PTRS);
  }
```

--> It also calls "dup_mmap()" to copy the VMAs

After copying all the process information, at last, the process is woken up :

```
wake_up_new_task(p);
```

MMU, page tables and page fault handling

Let us discuss more about the processes page tables, "task_struct -> mm_struct -> pgd". Every process's page table is referenced, modified and kept at this location. Initially when the process is created there is no physical page assigned to the process. Only the virtual addresses are allocated for a process.

Once a process tries to access a virtual address, the CPU looks in the page table/TLB for the physical address corresponding to it (i.e. looks up the relevant page table entry). Then it takes the physical address and puts it on the address bus. This can be depicted in the following diagram.

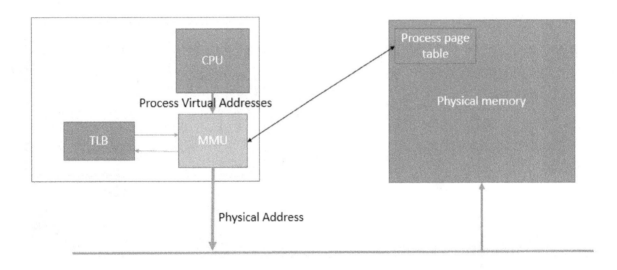

What if the virtual address to physical mapping is not there in the TLB?
If the mapping is not there in TLB and present in processes page tables then CPU fetches the mapping from the processes page tables and updates the TLB cache.

What if the virtual address to physical mapping is neither in the TLB nor in the page table?
If the mapping from VA to PA is not there in the page tables, then this case is known as a page fault. An exception (Page fault exception) is raised by the MMU.

This exception calls the "page_fault" handler.

Page fault handler walks through all the virtual memory areas, finds the VMA inside which the VA falls. It does this by comparing the VA with the start and end address of all the VMAs. If a VMA is found, then that is returned. If the VA is not in the range of any VMA then the page fault handler sends a SIGSEGV (segmentation fault) signal to the offending process.

If the address is valid then it allocates a physical page and updates the page table entries. This is known as demand paging. Demand paging does not require the entire process, that is, all pages of the process, to be in memory before the execution of the program begins.

The following diagram illustrates the same:

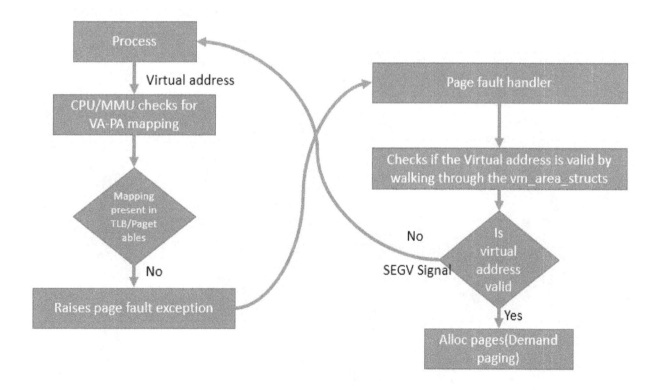

Chapter 4   Linux process scheduling

In this chapter lets go through the Linux scheduling internals. We will go through, Linux process states. Linux waitqueues, Linux scheduler classes, process run queues, Linux scheduler code and scheduler entry points

Linux process states

During its lifetime a Linux process keeps changing its state. While waiting for I/O to happen it may sleep. It may be waiting for the processor time slice to run.

All Linux process states are present in "sched.h". These can be following

```
#define  TASK_RUNNING            0x0000
#define  TASK_INTERRUPTIBLE      0x0001
#define  TASK_UNINTERRUPTIBLE        0x0002
#define  __TASK_STOPPED          0x0004
#define  __TASK_TRACED           0x0008
...
...
```

These are present in "task_struct->state". Majorly any process has the state as TASK_RUNNING. In this state the task can be currently executing or present in the runqueue for its turn to get the CPU.

We can say a process with TASK_RUNNING state can be scheduled anytime.

The 2 states of TASK_INTERRUPTIBLE and TASK_UNINTERRUPTIBLE are the waiting states. In these states the task is not scheduled. A task is put in these states if it is waiting for IO, or a condition is met, etc. We will shortly see how we can put a process in these states and how it comes out of these states.

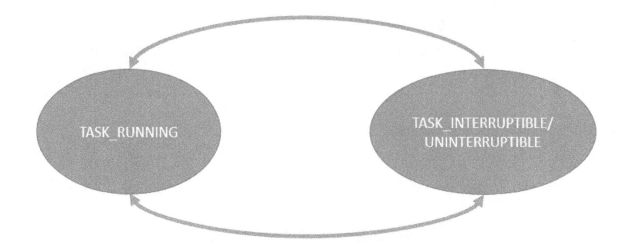

What is a way to come out of these sleeping states ?
We can wake up the process using "wake_up_process()" function.
"wake_up_process()" function sets the "task_struct->state" as TASK_RUNNING and puts it for scheduling.

Let's write a small program to create a kernel thread (a task) and put it to sleep. For putting it to sleep we set the state as TASK_UNINTERRUPTIBLE and call "schedule()".

```
printk(KERN_INFO "IN THREAD FUNCTION 1 \n");
set_current_state(TASK_UNINTERRUPTIBLE);
schedule();
printk(KERN_INFO "EXIT from thread function 1\n");
```

Next we send an IOCTL to this sleeping process and wake this process.
```
wake_up_process(sleeping_task);
```

The kernel module :
```
#include <linux/kernel.h>
#include <linux/module.h>
#include <linux/init.h>
```

```
#include <linux/types.h>
#include <linux/major.h>
#include <linux/fs.h>
#include <linux/device.h>
#include <linux/miscdevice.h>
#include <linux/kthread.h>
#include <asm/uaccess.h>


#define MY_MAGIC 'K'
#define CREATE_TASK _IOR(MY_MAGIC, 0, int)
#define WAKE_TASK _IOR(MY_MAGIC, 1, int)

struct task_struct *sleeping_task;

int thread_function_one(void *data)
{
        int ret = 10;
        printk(KERN_INFO "IN THREAD FUNCTION 1 \n");
        set_current_state(TASK_UNINTERRUPTIBLE);
        schedule();
        printk(KERN_INFO "EXIT from thread function 1\n");
        return ret;
}

void create_task(void)
{
        int cpu;
        int data;
        cpu = get_cpu();
        put_cpu();
        sleeping_task =
kthread_create_on_node(&thread_function_one,(void *)&data,
cpu_to_node(cpu), "our_thread");
        wake_up_process(sleeping_task);
}
```

```c
long trial_ioctl(struct file *file, unsigned int cmd,
unsigned long arg)
{
        switch(cmd) {
                case CREATE_TASK:
                        printk("create task ioctl\n");
                        create_task();
                        break;
                case WAKE_TASK:
                        printk("wake task ioctl\n");
                        wake_up_process(sleeping_task);
                        break;
                default:
                        return -ENOTTY;
        }
        return 0;
}


static const struct file_operations trial_fops={
        .owner = THIS_MODULE,
        .unlocked_ioctl = trial_ioctl
};

static struct miscdevice misc_struct={
        .minor = MISC_DYNAMIC_MINOR ,
        //a minor number is assigned - we can give our own
also , error if that's already taken
        .name = "trial_device",
        .fops = &trial_fops ,            //for the functions
of the char driver
};



static int __init func_init(void)
{
        int result = 0;
        printk(" In func_init () . module inserted .
Calling misc_register after this. \n");
```

```
        result = misc_register(&misc_struct) ;  // zero on
success ; neg error code on failure;other version :
register_chrdev
        if (result<0)
                printk("misc_register error ");
        else
                printk("device registered with minor number
= %i \n" , misc_struct.minor);
        return result ;
}

static void __exit func_exit(void)
{
        misc_deregister(&misc_struct) ;
        printk("device unregistered");
}

module_init(func_init);
module_exit(func_exit);

MODULE_AUTHOR("sampleauthor");
MODULE_DESCRIPTION("trial character driver");
MODULE_LICENSE("GPL");
```

The makefile for this:

```
obj-m+=device.o
KDIR=/lib/modules/$(shell uname -r)/build
all:
        $(MAKE) -C $(KDIR) SUBDIRS=$(PWD) modules
clean:
        rm -rf *.o *.ko *.mod.* .c* .t* .*.cmd
.tmp_versions
```

After inserting this kernel module we get a character device created in "/dev/" directory.

Complete user space program :

```c
#include <unistd.h>
#include <sys/types.h>
#include <sys/stat.h>
#include <sys/ioctl.h>
#include <fcntl.h>
#include <stdio.h>

#define MY_MAGIC 'K'
#define CREATE_TASK _IOR(MY_MAGIC, 0, int)
#define WAKE_TASK _IOR(MY_MAGIC, 1, int)


int main()
{
        int my_fd = -1, ret;
        unsigned char buf[11] = {0};
        ssize_t bytes = 0;

        my_fd = open("/dev/trial_device", O_RDWR);
        bytes = read(my_fd, buf, 10);
        printf("buf returned is %s\n", buf);

        printf("calling create task\n");
        ret = ioctl(my_fd, CREATE_TASK, NULL);
        sleep(10);
        printf("calling wake task\n");
        ret = ioctl(my_fd, WAKE_TASK, NULL);
        close(my_fd);

        return 0;
}
```

When the process is in TASK_UNINTERRUPTIBLE state we see that the output of "ps" command shows the state as 'D'.

Linux waitqueues and wakeup

In the previous section we see that the "sleeping_task" variable is a global variable where we store the "task_struct" of the newly created task. We use this saved "task_struct" to wake the process whenever we need.

Now let's assume we want many processes waiting/sleeping and we want to wake them all at once. In such a case we would have to save pointers of all the "task_structs" of the sleeping process, somewhere, say in a linked list. Such linked lists, which saves the sleeping "task_structs" are known as waitqueues.

All the processes in wait queues can be woken up when a condition is met. Let's see the standard Linux waitqueue:

The waitqueue structure is :

```
struct __wait_queue {
        unsigned int            flags;
        void                    *private;
        wait_queue_func_t       func;
        struct list_head        task_list;
};
typedef struct __wait_queue wait_queue_t;
```

Basically, it has a "wait_queue" function and a "task_list".

There are generic functions to add the processes task_struct to this task_list.
Lets see the basic implementation of "__add_wait_queue()".
Tasks are added to the list using add_wait_queue:

```
static inline void __add_wait_queue(wait_queue_head_t
*head, wait_queue_t *new)
{
        list_add(&new->task_list, &head->task_list);
}
```

Other functions which are wrappers above these are:

```
#define wait_event_interruptible(wq, condition)
#define wait_event_timeout(wq, condition, timeout) { ... }
```

```
#define wait_event_interruptible_timeout(wq, condition,
timeout)
```

Adding to waitqueue is done by the above functions. Some point of time these tasks need to be woken up with the help of "wake_up" functions.

```
include/linux/wait.h
#define wake_up(x) __wake_up(x, TASK_UNINTERRUPTIBLE |
TASK_INTERRUPTIBLE, 1, NULL)
#define wake_up_nr(x, nr) __wake_up(x, TASK_UNINTERRUPTIBLE
| TASK_INTERRUPTIBLE, nr, NULL)
#define wake_up_all(x) __wake_up(x, TASK_UNINTERRUPTIBLE |
TASK_INTERRUPTIBLE, 0, NULL)
#define wake_up_interruptible(x) __wake_up(x,
TASK_INTERRUPTIBLE, 1, NULL)
#define wake_up_interruptible_nr(x, nr) __wake_up(x,
TASK_INTERRUPTIBLE, nr, NULL)
#define wake_up_interruptible_all(x) __wake_up(x,
TASK_INTERRUPTIBLE, 0, NULL)
```

Linux Scheduler classes

In Linux, scheduling is determined by the scheduling class to which the process belongs. The common structure for the scheduler class is "struct sched_class" defined in "kernel/sched/sched.h".

```
struct sched_class {
    const struct sched_class *next;
    void (*enqueue_task) (struct rq *rq, struct task_struct
*p, int flags);
    void (*dequeue_task) (struct rq *rq, struct task_struct
*p, int flags);
    void (*yield_task) (struct rq *rq);
    bool (*yield_to_task) (struct rq *rq, struct
task_struct *p, bool preempt);
```

```
    void (*check_preempt_curr) (struct rq *rq, struct
task_struct *p, int flags);
...

...

    struct task_struct * (*pick_next_task) (struct rq *rq,
    struct task_struct *prev, struct rq_flags *rf);
    void (*put_prev_task) (struct rq *rq, struct
task_struct *p);

#ifdef CONFIG_SMP
    int   (*select_task_rq)(struct task_struct *p, int
task_cpu, int sd_flag, int flags);
    void (*migrate_task_rq)(struct task_struct *p);
    void (*task_woken) (struct rq *this_rq, struct
task_struct *task);
    void (*set_cpus_allowed)(struct task_struct *p,  const
struct cpumask *newmask);
    void (*rq_online)(struct rq *rq);
    void (*rq_offline)(struct rq *rq);
#endif

    void (*set_curr_task) (struct rq *rq);
    void (*task_tick) (struct rq *rq, struct task_struct
*p, int queued);
    void (*task_fork) (struct task_struct *p);
    void (*task_dead) (struct task_struct *p);


...

    void (*update_curr) (struct rq *rq);
...
...
};
```

All existing scheduling classes in the kernel are in a list.

stop_sched_class → rt_sched_class → fair_sched_class → idle_sched_class

→ NULL

This linked list defines a priority among scheduler classes. The highest priority scheduler class that has a runnable process wins.

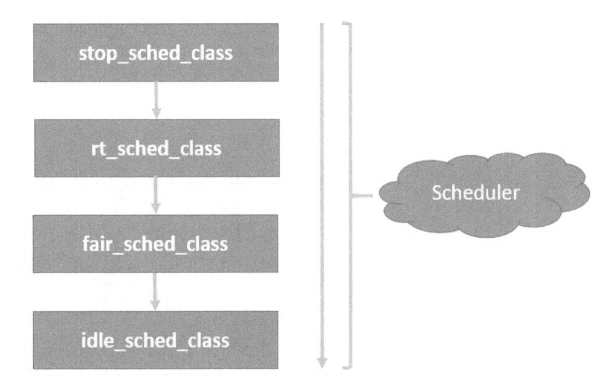

Let's see in actual code how things happen. The scheduling is done by "__schedule()" function. It calls the "pick_next_task()" function to find the next task to be run.

```
__schedule {
..
next = pick_next_task(rq, prev, &rf);
..
}
```

The pick_next_task in turn iterates through all the scheduler classes in order of the linked list mentioned above.
Let's see the "pick_next_task()" function:
```
pick_next_task(struct rq *rq, struct task_struct *prev,
struct rq_flags *rf)
```

```
{
..
    for_each_class(class) {
        p = class->pick_next_task(rq, prev, rf);
        if (p) {
            if (unlikely(p == RETRY_TASK))
                goto again;
            return p;
        }
    }
..
}


#define for_each_class(class) \
    for (class = sched_class_highest; class; class = class->next)
```

One more thing to notice here is that "idle_sched_class" will always have a runnable process. When nothing is running, the idle process runs :-)
Can we enter a power saving mode when an idle task is running?
Yes!!

Let's see the implementation of the idle task :
```
arch/x86/kernel/process.c
void __cpuidle default_idle(void)
{
    trace_cpu_idle_rcuidle(1, smp_processor_id());
    safe_halt();
    trace_cpu_idle_rcuidle(PWR_EVENT_EXIT,
smp_processor_id());
}


/*
 * Used in the idle loop; sti takes one instruction cycle
 * to complete:
 */
static inline __cpuidle void arch_safe_halt(void)
```

```
{
        native_safe_halt();
}

static inline __cpuidle void native_safe_halt(void)
{
        asm volatile("sti; hlt": : :"memory");
}
```

HLT instruction : HLT (halt) is an assembly language instruction which halts the central processing unit (CPU) until the next external interrupt is fired. The HLT instruction cuts the power usage.

In short we can say that if none of the scheduler classes has a runnable process then idle task takes over and saves power.

Details of the scheduling classes

Stop and Idle are special scheduling classes. Stop is used to schedule the per-cpu stop task. It preempts everything and can be preempted by nothing, and Idle is used to schedule the per-cpu idle task (also called swapper task) which is run if no other task is runnable. The other two are for real time (rt_sched_class) and normal tasks (fair_sched_class).

"kernel\sched\fair.c" implements the CFS scheduler described above.
Fair_sched_class

"kernel\sched\rt.c" implements SCHED_FIFO and SCHED_RR semantics
rt_sched_class

Scheduler class is present in the "task_struct" of a process.
```
struct task_struct {
  ..
  int prio, static_prio, normal_prio;
  unsigned int rt_priority;
  const struct sched_class *sched_class;
  struct sched_entity se;
  struct sched_rt_entity rt;
```

```
#ifdef CONFIG_CGROUP_SCHED
 struct task_group *sched_task_group;
#endif
 struct sched_dl_entity dl;
...
}
```

Where are the scheduler classes assigned to a process ?

The task struct is initialized with "sched_class" when a process is forked

```
sched_fork() {
...
} else if (rt_prio(p->prio)) {
  p->sched_class = &rt_sched_class;
 } else {
  p->sched_class = &fair_sched_class;
 }
...
}
```

Runqueues

The basic data structure in the scheduler is the runqueue. The runqueue is defined in "kernel/sched.c" as "struct rq". The runqueue is the list of runnable processes on a given processor; there is one "runqueue" per processor.

runqueue data structures for fair and real time scheduling classes
struct cfs_rq cfs;
struct rt_rq rt;

Scheduler and its entry points

Where is the scheduler code (is it a process??)

In Linux the scheduling is done by a piece of code. This code is actually a function "__schedule()". This code is executed at places called as entry points.

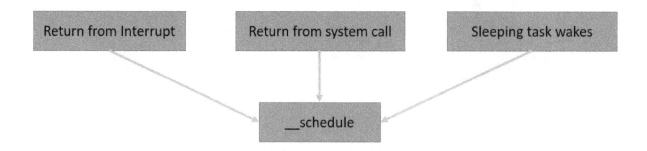

Return from Interrupt Entry point

One of the entry points of the scheduler is interrupts. That is whenever an interrupt occurs, the interrupt handler is executed. After the interrupt handler is executed "ret_from_intr()" function is executed in the "ret_from_intr()" function "__schedule()" is called.

This makes sure that scheduling is done after every interrupt.

Upon returning from a hardware interrupt, the "need_resched" flag is checked. If it is set and "preempt_count" is zero (meaning we're in a preemptible region of the kernel and no locks are held), the kernel invokes the scheduler.

While returning from interrupt in **entry_64.S** function :

```
/* Interrupt entry/exit. */
common_interrupt:
    addq $-0x80, (%rsp)                /* Adjust vector to [-
256, -1] range */
    call interrupt_entry
    UNWIND_HINT_REGS indirect=1
    call do_IRQ    /* rdi points to pt_regs */
    /* 0(%rsp): old RSP */
ret_from_intr:
...
/* Returning to kernel space */
retint_kernel:
#ifdef CONFIG_PREEMPT
    /* Interrupts are off */
    /* Check if we need preemption */
```

```
        btl  $9, EFLAGS(%rsp)          /* were interrupts off? */
        jnc  1f
0:      cmpl $0, PER_CPU_VAR(__preempt_count)
        jnz  1f
        call preempt_schedule_irq
```

Preempt_schedule_irq implementation:

```
 void __sched preempt_schedule_irq(void)
  {
  ...
  local_irq_enable();
  __schedule();
  local_irq_disable();
  ...
  }
```

We can ask that if none of the interrupts are occurring then we will never schedule out the current process ?
Timer interrupt comes to the rescue.
There is a timer interrupt which gets invoked at regular intervals. Even if none of the other interrupts occur, the timer interrupt occurs after a specific period. At the end of the timer interrupt the "__schedule()" is called.

Return to user-space (system call return path)

Snippet from entry_64.S

System call entry :
```
GLOBAL(entry_SYSCALL_64_after_hwframe)


..
        call do_syscall_64      /* returns with IRQs disabled */
...
jne  swapgs_restore_regs_and_return_to_usermode
```

```
...
...
GLOBAL(swapgs_restore_regs_and_return_to_usermode)
..
..

    call preempt_schedule_irq
...
```

Sleeping task wakes up

The code that causes an event to wake up the sleeping task typically calls "wake_up()" on the corresponding wait queue which eventually ends up in the scheduler function "try_to_wake_up()".

```
#define wake_up(x)                        __wake_up(x,
TASK_NORMAL, 1, NULL)
__wake_up ->
__wake_up_common_lock->
__wake_up_common->
ret = curr->func(curr, mode, wake_flags, key)->
autoremove_wake_function->
default_wake_function->
try_to_wake_up ->
ttwu_queue ->
ttwu_do_activate- >
ttwu_activate ->
activate_task->
enqueue_task->
p->sched_class->enqueue_task(rq, p, flags);
```

Chapter 5   Linux Interrupts

In this chapter we will go through meaning of hardware interrupt, registration of interrupt handlers and complete flow of interrupt handler execution.

What is interrupt

In this section we will look at interrupts. In this chapter, the reference to "interrupt" implies reference to a hardware interrupt.
An interrupt is a signal at the CPU pin INT. The interrupt from a device is an electronic signal which is edge triggered, level triggered, active high or active low.

For all these hardware signals are received from devices to the programmable interrupt controller(PIC). The PIC then sends a single signal to the CPU INT pin. When a CPU INT pin receives the signal from PIC, it executes the current instruction and jumps to a code location which is common for all interrupts.

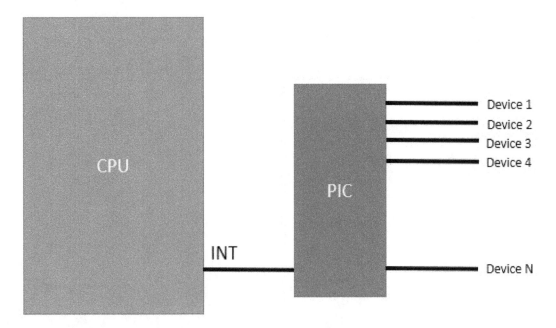

Among all the devices attached to the PIC, it decides which interrupt shall be given to the CPU. After the CPU receives a signal at the INT pin, it reads the hardware register of the PIC to see the interrupt number. The unique interrupt number is used to determine, which device has raised the interrupt.

After the device is determined, the CPU will execute the interrupt handler registered for the device.

Interrupt handler registration

Interrupt handler is registered for a device's interrupt using the "request_irq()" function.

request_irq(unsigned int irq, irq_handler_t handler, unsigned long flags,
        const char *name, void *dev)

Every interrupt has an **interrupt descriptor** associated with it. Let's see the descriptor for a particular interrupt.

Interrupt descriptor.
```
struct irq_desc {
        struct irq_common_data  irq_common_data;
        struct irq_data         irq_data;
        unsigned int __percpu   *kstat_irqs;
        irq_flow_handler_t      handle_irq;
#ifdef CONFIG_IRQ_PREFLOW_FASTEOI
    irq_preflow_handler_t  preflow_handler;
#endif
    struct irqaction    *action; /* IRQ action list */
    unsigned int        status_use_accessors;
    unsigned int
    core_internal_state__do_not_mess_with_it;
    unsigned int        depth;          /* nested irq disables
*/
    unsigned int        wake_depth;   /* nested wake enables
*/
    unsigned int        irq_count;    /* For detecting broken
IRQs */
    ...
```

```
...
#ifdef CONFIG_PROC_FS
     struct proc_dir_entry   *dir;
#endif
     int             parent_irq;
     struct module       *owner;
     const char          *name;
} ____cacheline_internodeal
```

We see that the interrupt handler function pointer list is also present in irq_desc :

```
struct irqaction  *action; /* IRQ action list */
```

SHARED interrupt handlers

"struct irqaction" list has more than one element if the interrupt is shared between multiple devices. The interrupt handlers are added to this list. When an interrupt is shared between devices then the registration is done multiple times by the different devices' device drivers.

When an interrupt occurs for a device then the shared handlers are executed serially.

Below is the code where the list of interrupt handlers are executed. We see that as long as IRQ_HANDLED is returned by each of the handlers, all the handlers in the list are executed.

The following function illustrates how all the handlers(action list) are executed for a particular interrupt. The implementation is present in "__handle_irq_event_percpu()" function.

```
irqreturn_t __handle_irq_event_percpu(struct irq_desc
*desc, unsigned int *flags)
{
        irqreturn_t retval = IRQ_NONE;
        unsigned int irq = desc->irq_data.irq;
        struct irqaction *action;
```

```
        record_irq_time(desc);

        for_each_action_of_desc(desc, action) {
                irqreturn_t res;
                trace_irq_handler_entry(irq, action);
                res = action->handler(irq, action->dev_id);
                trace_irq_handler_exit(irq, action, res);

                if (WARN_ONCE(!irqs_disabled(),"irq %u
handler %pF enabled interrupts\n",
                                irq, action->handler))
                        local_irq_disable();
                switch (res) {
...
...
...

                default:
                        break;
                }
                retval |= res;
        }
        return retval;
}
```

Enabling and disabling of interrupts

The functions for enabling and disabling interrupts are "enable_irq()" and "disable_irq()". These functions enable or disable interrupts from the Programmable interrupt controller (PIC).

Let's see an implementation of "enable_irq()" from the kernel source :
"enable_irq()" calls "__enable_irq()" with the irq number. It finally calls "irq_enable()" function and we see a call as below :

```
if (desc->irq_data.chip->irq_enable) {
    desc->irq_data.chip->irq_enable(&desc->irq_data);
    irq_state_clr_masked(desc);
```

```
}
```

We see that "irq_enable" and "irq_unmask" are Programmable interrupt controller specific functions.

```
static struct irq_chip irq_type_iosapic_edge = {
        .name =                     "IO-SAPIC-edge",
        .irq_startup =              iosapic_startup_edge_irq,
        .irq_shutdown =             iosapic_disable_edge_irq,
        .irq_enable =               iosapic_enable_edge_irq,
        .irq_disable =              iosapic_disable_edge_irq,
        .irq_ack =                  iosapic_ack_edge_irq,
        .irq_mask =                 mask_irq,
        .irq_unmask =               unmask_irq,
        .irq_set_affinity =         iosapic_set_affinity
};
```

Hence it is clear that enabling and disabling of interrupts is done in the PIC.

We have another set of functions which disable/enable interrupts for the current CPU. The disabling is done by executing a code at the CPU. These functions are "local_irq_disable()" and "local_irq_enable()". Lets see the implementation of these functions:

```
#define local_irq_enable()  do { raw_local_irq_enable(); }
while (0)
#define local_irq_disable() do { raw_local_irq_disable(); }
while (0)
```

Definition of **raw_local_irq_enable**
```
#define raw_local_irq_enable() arch_local_irq_enable()
```

```
static inline notrace void arch_local_irq_enable(void)
{
```

```
        native_irq_enable();
}
```

```
static inline void native_irq_disable(void)
{
    asm volatile("cli": : :"memory");
}
```

Disabling the interrupts this way means that we are disabling the interrupts from the current processor. We are just invoking the CLI (clear interrupt) instruction.

CLI only affects the interrupt flag for the processor on which it is executed. This clears the interrupt flag.

Similarly enabling the interrupt is done by STI (set interrupt) instruction.

```
static inline void native_irq_enable(void)
{
    asm volatile("sti": : :"memory");
}
```

There is one more variation where we save the flags while disabling and restore the flags after
```
local_irq_save(flags)
local_irq_restore(flags)
```

Interrupt handling and execution

Let's see how interrupts are handled in the x86 system. On every interrupt the "do_IRQ()" function is called. do_IRQ() function implementation is present in file "arch/x86/kernel/entry_64.S".
```
...
...
common_interrupt:
    addq $-0x80, (%rsp)                    /* Adjust vector to [-
256, -1] range */
```

```
call interrupt_entry
UNWIND_HINT_REGS indirect=1
call do_IRQ    /* rdi points to pt_regs */
/* 0(%rsp): old RSP */
```
...
...

The "do_IRQ()" implementation first enters into the interrupt context using the function "irq_enter()". (arch/x86/kernel/irq.c).

The function "irq_enter()" does many things with timers. It also increments the preempt count :
```
preempt_count_add(HARDIRQ_OFFSET);
```

"do_IRQ()" function fetches the interrupt number from the CPU register and extracts the interrupt descriptor from the interrupt descriptor table.
```
        unsigned vector = ~regs->orig_ax;
..
        desc = __this_cpu_read(vector_irq[vector]);
```

There is one interrupt descriptor corresponding to each interrupt. Among many things Interrupt descriptor has interrupt handlers for an interrupt. After fetching the interrupt descriptor, things are set to execute the interrupt handler. It is done in the "handle_irq()" function.
"handle_irq()" calls "generic_handle_irq_desc()".

```
static inline void generic_handle_irq_desc(unsigned int
irq, struct irq_desc *desc)
{
 desc->handle_irq(irq, desc);
}
```

generic_handle_irq_desc function calls handle_irq for this descriptor:
```
desc->handle_irq(irq, desc);
```

For an interrupt descriptor, "handle_irq()" would have been set by "irq_set_chip_and_handler_name()" at the time of initialization.

Generally this will point to "handle_edge_irq()" or "handle_level_irq()". These functions are set depending upon if the interrupt getting handled is level triggered or edge.

Difference between Edge and Level triggered interrupt

We shall see the implementation of "handle_edge_irq()" and "handle_level_irq()". On looking into the details, we see that amongst these two types of handlers, edge triggered interrupts are not masked while the handler is executing. On the other hand level triggered interrupts are masked when the interrupt handler is executed.

Edge triggered IRQs can be handled with the level-triggered descriptor, but that has slightly more overhead. Level-triggered interrupts cannot be handled with the edge-triggered handler, without risking IRQ storms and other ugly races.

Handle_irq_event

Independent of these handlings, "handle_irq_event()" function is called for executing an interrupt handler.

handle_irq_event : This function runs all the handlers registered with this interrupt

handle_irq_event()   -->   handle_irq_event_percpu()   -->
__handle_irq_event_percpu()

```
__handle_irq_event_percpu
{

  do {
        ...
          res = action->handler(irq, action->dev_id);
```

```
    ...
    ...
        switch (res) {
    ...
    ...
      case IRQ_HANDLED:
    ...
    ...
        action = action->next;
    ...
    } while (action);
}
```

This is the case of shared handlers where if one irq line is shared for many devices then all the interrupt handlers are executed one by one.

End of Interrupt

The APIC on x86 systems has to send the #EOI signal on the PCI bus to tell that interrupt processing is completed. This is done just after the irq is handled in the "do_IRQ()" function.

```
do_IRQ()
...
 if (!handle_irq(irq, regs)) {
  ack_APIC_irq();
...
```

All these function calls can be depicted by following figure :

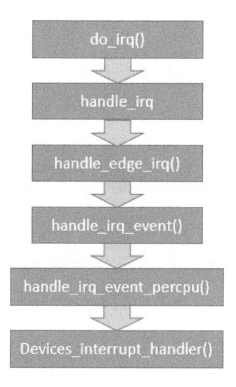

Ftrace of do_irq function

The following ftrace graph on "do_IRQ()" function will show you the sequence of events, This is interrupt handling for a mouse interrupt :

```
1)     ==========>  |
1)                  |  do_IRQ() {
1)                  |    irq_enter() {
1)                  |      rcu_irq_enter() {
1)    0.201 us      |        rcu_eqs_exit_common.isra.45();
1)    1.223 us      |      }
1)                  |      tick_irq_enter() {
1)    0.190 us      |
tick_check_oneshot_broadcast_this_cpu();
1)                  |        ktime_get() {
1)    1.192 us      |          read_hpet();
1)    2.174 us      |        }
1)                  |        update_ts_time_stats() {
1)    0.175 us      |          nr_iowait_cpu();
```

```
1)    1.217 us     |               }
1)                 |               ktime_get() {
1)    1.057 us     |                 read_hpet();
1)    2.019 us     |               }
1)    0.135 us     |               touch_softlockup_watchdog();
1)                 |               tick_do_update_jiffies64() {
1)    0.185 us     |                 _raw_spin_lock();
1)                 |                 do_timer() {
1)    0.140 us     |                   calc_global_load();
1)    1.162 us     |                 }
1)    0.135 us     |                 _raw_spin_unlock();
1)                 |                 update_wall_time() {
1)    0.200 us     |                   _raw_spin_lock_irqsave();
1)    0.967 us     |                   read_hpet();
1)    0.140 us     |                   ntp_tick_length();
1)    0.136 us     |                   ntp_tick_length();
1)    0.136 us     |                   ntp_tick_length();
1)                 |
timekeeping_update.constprop.8() {
1)    0.290 us     |                     update_vsyscall();
1)                 |                     raw_notifier_call_chain()
{
1)    0.246 us     |                       notifier_call_chain();
1)    1.193 us     |                     }
1)    3.526 us     |                   }
1)    0.191 us     |
_raw_spin_unlock_irqrestore();
1) + 11.778 us     |                 }
1) + 16.802 us     |               }
1)    0.135 us     |               touch_softlockup_watchdog();
1) + 29.011 us     |             }
1)                 |             _local_bh_enable() {
1)    0.145 us     |               __local_bh_enable();
1)    1.107 us     |             }
1) + 34.723 us     |           }
1)                 |           exit_idle() {
1)                 |             atomic_notifier_call_chain() {
1)    0.145 us     |               notifier_call_chain();
```

```
 1)    1.107 us    |            }
 1)    2.069 us    |          }
 1)                |        handle_irq() {
 1)    0.225 us    |          irq_to_desc();
 1)                |          handle_edge_irq() {
 1)    0.175 us    |            _raw_spin_lock();
 1)    0.180 us    |            irq_may_run();
 1)                |            apic_ack_edge() {
 1)    0.140 us    |              irq_complete_move();
 1)    0.140 us    |              irq_move_irq();
 1)    2.069 us    |            }
 1)                |            handle_irq_event() {
 1)    0.140 us    |              _raw_spin_unlock();
 1)                |              handle_irq_event_percpu() {
 1)                |                i8042_interrupt() {
 1)    0.231 us    |                  _raw_spin_lock_irqsave();
 1)    0.155 us    |
_raw_spin_unlock_irqrestore();
 1)                |                  serio_interrupt() {
 1)    0.205 us    |
_raw_spin_lock_irqsave();
 1)                |                    psmouse_interrupt
[psmouse]() {
 1)                |                      psmouse_handle_byte
[psmouse]() {
 1)    0.315 us    |
synaptics_process_byte [psmouse]();
 1)    1.303 us    |                      }
 1)    2.390 us    |                    }
 1)    0.210 us    |
_raw_spin_unlock_irqrestore();
 1)    5.816 us    |                  }
 1) + 14.528 us    |                }
 1)    0.340 us    |                add_interrupt_randomness();
 1)    0.196 us    |                note_interrupt();
 1) + 18.517 us    |              }
 1)    0.196 us    |              _raw_spin_lock();
 1) + 21.462 us    |            }
```

```
1)    0.150 us    |             _raw_spin_unlock();
1) + 28.525 us    |           }
1) + 30.554 us    |         }
1)                |         irq_exit() {
1)    0.165 us    |           idle_cpu();
1)                |           tick_nohz_irq_exit() {
1)                |             __tick_nohz_idle_enter() {
1)                |               ktime_get() {
1)    1.298 us    |                 read_hpet();
1)    2.340 us    |               }
1)    0.151 us    |               timekeeping_max_deferment();
1)                |               get_next_timer_interrupt() {
1)    0.206 us    |                 _raw_spin_lock();
1)    0.151 us    |                 _raw_spin_unlock();
1)                |                 hrtimer_get_next_event() {
1)    0.191 us    |                   _raw_spin_lock_irqsave();
1)    0.151 us    |
_raw_spin_unlock_irqrestore();
1)    2.109 us    |                 }
1)    5.100 us    |               }
1)                |               hrtimer_start() {
1)                |                 __hrtimer_start_range_ns() {
1)                |
lock_hrtimer_base.isra.22() {
1)    0.180 us    |
_raw_spin_lock_irqsave();
1)    1.147 us    |                 }
1)    0.246 us    |                 __remove_hrtimer();
1)    0.135 us    |                 get_nohz_timer_target();
1)    0.321 us    |                 enqueue_hrtimer();
1)    0.156 us    |
_raw_spin_unlock_irqrestore();
1)    6.373 us    |                 }
1)    7.329 us    |               }
1) + 18.691 us    |             }
1) + 19.658 us    |           }
1)                |           rcu_irq_exit() {
1)    0.225 us    |             rcu_eqs_enter_common.isra.44();
```

```
1)     1.277 us     |         }
1)  + 23.781 us     |      }
1)  + 94.920 us     |    }
1)     <========== |
```

Chapter 6   Signals Internals

Introduction

A signal is one of the simpler and basic forms of IPC (Inter-process communication), with a precise goal. A "signal" is sent to a process notifying about an event, and to instruct/force it to take a specific action. These actions can be default actions for specific signals, or custom ones which do user defined tasks.

Every signal in the kernel is assigned a unique numeric value. This numeric value is used to identify the signal. These values might be different for different architectures. Some signals and their numeric values are mentioned below (for x86 architecture). You can explore more signals using the bash command "kill -l".

Signal	Numeric value
SIGINT	2
SIGQUIT	3
SIGKILL	9
SIGSEGV	11
SIGPIPE	13
SIGTERM	15
SIGSTOP	19

Internally signals are divided into synchronous and asynchronous signals. Synchronous signals are ones which are sent to the process from within itself. Signals like SIGSEGV, SIGBUS are synchronous signals.There is a macro in the kernel which controls this.

```
#define SYNCHRONOUS_MASK \
    (sigmask(SIGSEGV) | sigmask(SIGBUS) | sigmask(SIGILL) |
\
```

```
        sigmask(SIGTRAP) | sigmask(SIGFPE) | sigmask(SIGSYS))
```

On the other hand, asynchronous signals are ones which are sent to the process from outside, that is, from other processes.

The design and working of signals is very simple. When a signal is sent to a process, it is delivered to it, and the process remembers it through its internal data structures. At an appropriate time the process checks for any pending signals that it has and processes them. The processing would involve calling a specific signal handler for that signal. We will discuss all of this in detail later in this chapter.

Every thread/process keeps track of data related to signal processing through a number of member structures in its "task_struct" structure.

The first one is a pointer to the structure "struct signal_struct". It mainly stores information related to shared signals, which are shared by the process/thread group (identified using PGID/TGID) which the process belongs to. Besides this, it stores a number of fields which are not strictly related to the signal IPC, hence we will skip these for now.

Another important structure stored in "task_struct" is a pointer to the structure "struct sighand_struct". This contains information related to signal handlers. Signal handlers are functions which are called when a signal is delivered to a process. The structure "sighand_struct" contains an array of type "struct k_sigaction".

```
struct sighand_struct {
    atomic_t        count;
    struct k_sigaction  action[_NSIG];
    spinlock_t      siglock;
    wait_queue_head_t   signalfd_wqh;
};

struct k_sigaction {
    struct sigaction sa;
    .

    .
```

```
};
```

The structure "k_sigaction" contains the structure "sigaction" as its member. This "sigaction" structure contains the signal handlers which are pointers to functions.

```
struct sigaction {
#ifndef __ARCH_HAS_IRIX_SIGACTION
    __sighandler_t  sa_handler;
    unsigned long   sa_flags;
#else
    unsigned int  sa_flags;
    __sighandler_t  sa_handler;
#endif
    .

    .

};
```

Let us ignore the architecture specific difference in that structure. By default, the "sa_handler" field is populated with default signal handlers. But this can be changed to a custom signal handler. We will explore this idea later and see how the kernel updates this signal handler.

The last data structure which we shall discuss here is the structure "sigpending". A pointer to this structure exists in the "task_struct" of the process.

```
struct sigpending {
    struct list_head list;
    sigset_t signal;
};
```

The "list" structure inside "sigpending" contains the list of pending signals for this process. The members of the "list" structure are of the type "struct sigqueue".

```
struct sigqueue {
```

```
      struct list_head list;
      int flags;
      kernel_siginfo_t info;
      struct user_struct *user;
};
```

When a signal is to be enqueued into the "sigpending" structure, a new "sigqueue" structure is created, and updated with the related fields. It is then added to the tail of the above mentioned "list". The main member of the structure "sigqueue" is the "kernel_siginfo_t" structure. This holds all the relevant information.

```
typedef struct kernel_siginfo {
    __SIGINFO;
} kernel_siginfo_t;

#define __SIGINFO                    \
struct {                     \
    int si_signo;                \
    int si_errno;            \
    int si_code;             \
    union __sifields _sifields; \
}
```

In the "kernel_siginfo_t" structure, "si_signo" stores the signal number of the pending signal. Other fields include "si_errno" which stores the error status, "si_code" which is basically used to notify some information related to the signal. For example, this information can be the origin of the signal (kernel, or user). The union "__sifields" contains more detailed information such as the pid of the process, etc. We will not go into the details of this union here.

Signal Delivery

Let us discuss the most popular ways of sending a signal to a process. The "kill" system call. There are other ways of sending a signal, but we will discuss how the "kill" system call delivers the signal to the process. You will see later that some of the other ways also take the same execution path after a certain point.

The kill system call takes two parameters, the "pid" of the process to which the signal is to be delivered, and the numeric value of the signal to be delivered.

```
int kill (pid_t pid, int sig);
```

The definition of the "kill" system call looks something like this.

```
SYSCALL_DEFINE2(kill, pid_t, pid, int, sig)
{
    struct kernel_siginfo info;

    clear_siginfo(&info);
    info.si_signo = sig;
    info.si_errno = 0;
    info.si_code = SI_USER;
    info.si_pid = task_tgid_vnr(current);
    info.si_uid = from_kuid_munged(current_user_ns(),
current_uid());

    return kill_something_info(sig, &info, pid);
}
```

It first creates a "kernel_siginfo" structure and updates the relevant fields with the details. The "si_code" is set to "SI_USER" as this signal is being sent through the "kill" system call. Sometimes signals are sent from within the kernel. For example, when the OOM (out of memory) killer sends a SIGKILL, the "si_code" ends up getting updated to "SI_KERNEL".
The function "kill_something_info()" is called.

The function "kill_something_info()" does the job of interpreting the pid passed to the kill system call. The pid passed to the kill system call can be interpreted in one of the three ways, as seen in the function definition of "kill_something_info()".

```
static int kill_something_info(int sig, struct kernel_siginfo
*info, pid_t pid)
{
    int ret;

    if (pid > 0) {
        rcu_read_lock();
        ret = kill_pid_info(sig, info, find_vpid(pid));
        rcu_read_unlock();
        return ret;
    }
    .
    .


    if (pid != -1) {
        ret = __kill_pgrp_info(sig, info,
                pid ? find_vpid(-pid) :
task_pgrp(current));
    } else {
            .
        for_each_process(p) {
                if (task_pid_vnr(p) > 1 &&
                    !same_thread_group(p, current)) {
                        int err =
group_send_sig_info(sig, info, p,
                                        PIDTYPE_MAX);
                    ++count;
                if (err != -EPERM)
                    retval = err;
                }
            }
        .
        .
}
```

The first "if" statement checks if the pid is positive. In case the pid sent to the kill system call is positive, then the signal is sent to only the process with ID specified by pid. For this the function "kill_pid_info()" is called.

The second "if" statement checks if the pid is not equal to -1. This would mean that the "if" statement will be executed when the pid is either equal to 0, or if its lesser than -1 (since positive pids are covered in the previous "if" statement). When the pid sent to a kill system call is 0, then the signal is sent to every process in the process group of the calling program. And when the pid is less than -1, then the signal is sent to every process in the process group whose ID is equal to -pid. This distinction is made with the ternary operator. In this execution path the function "__kill_pgrp_info()" is called.

The else block executes for cases when the pid sent to the kill system call is -1. In this call the signal is sent to all the processes to whom the calling process has the permission to send a signal. Here, the function "group_send_sig_info()" is called. As we discuss further, you will notice that the functions mentioned above also end up calling "group_send_sig_info()", but with a different parameter.

Let us talk about the functions called above one by one. The function "kill_pid_info()" takes the pid, fetches the "task_struct" structure for that process and calls "group_send_sig_info()".

```
int  kill_pid_info(int  sig,  struct  kernel_siginfo  *info,
struct pid *pid)
{
    int error = -ESRCH;
    struct task_struct *p;

    for (;;) {
        .
        if (p)
                    error = group_send_sig_info(sig,
info, p, PIDTYPE_TGID);
        .

        .

    }
```

```
}
```

The infinite for loop is present to take care of the case when the delivery of the signal fails for some reason. The "PIDTYPE_TGID" macro indicates that the pid being passed is that of a process. TGID is the pid of the whole process, while PID is the per thread pid. We will discuss the function "group_send_sig_info()" in a bit.

The function "__kill_pgrp_info()", which is called in the second if block, uses a loop to iterate over all the processes in that process group and calls "group_send_sig_info()" on them.

```
int __kill_pgrp_info(int sig, struct kernel_siginfo *info,
struct pid *pgrp)
{
    struct task_struct *p = NULL;
    int retval, success;

    success = 0;
    retval = -ESRCH;
    do_each_pid_task(pgrp, PIDTYPE_PGID, p) {
        int err = group_send_sig_info(sig, info, p,
PIDTYPE_PGID);
        success |= !err;
        retval = err;
    } while_each_pid_task(pgrp, PIDTYPE_PGID, p);
    return success ? 0 : retval;
}
```

Notice that the "PIDTYPE" here is "PIDTYPE_PGID", which indicates that pid being sent here is that of a group.

The else block of the above function "kill_something_info()" directly calls the function "group_send_sig_info()", for every process that the current process has the permission to send a signal to. It checks this by comparing the "signal" structure in the "task_struct" of the processes.

Now, let us take a look into the function "group_send_sig_info()".

```
int group_send_sig_info(int sig, struct kernel_siginfo
*info,
        struct task_struct *p, enum pid_type type)
{
    int ret;

    rcu_read_lock();
    ret = check_kill_permission(sig, info, p);
    rcu_read_unlock();

    if (!ret && sig)
        ret = do_send_sig_info(sig, info, p, type);

    return ret;
}
```

It first checks if the current process has the permission to send a signal to the process denoted by "p". It then calls "do_send_sig_info()" with the relevant parameters.

The function "do_send_sig_info()" just takes a lock on the "sighand" structure and calls the function "send_signal()".

```
int do_send_sig_info(int sig, struct kernel_siginfo *info,
struct task_struct *p,
        enum pid_type type)
{
    unsigned long flags;
    int ret = -ESRCH;

    if (lock_task_sighand(p, &flags)) {
        ret = send_signal(sig, info, p, type);
        unlock_task_sighand(p, &flags);
    }
```

```
        return ret;
}
```

The function "send_signal()", along with doing a bunch of other things, calls the function "__send_signal()".

The function "__send_signal()" performs the main task of creating the "sigqueue" structure, and enqueueing it to the "pending" (or "shared_pending" of the "signal" structure) structure of the "task_struct".

```
static int __send_signal(int sig, struct kernel_siginfo
*info, struct task_struct *t,
        enum pid_type type, int from_ancestor_ns)
{
    struct sigpending *pending;
    struct sigqueue *q;
    .

    .


    pending = (type != PIDTYPE_PID) ? &t->signal-
>shared_pending : &t->pending;
    .

    .


    q = __sigqueue_alloc(sig, t, GFP_ATOMIC,
override_rlimit);
    if (q) {
        list_add_tail(&q->list, &pending->list);
        switch ((unsigned long) info) {
        case (unsigned long) SEND_SIG_NOINFO:
                clear_siginfo(&q->info);
                q->info.si_signo = sig;
                q->info.si_errno = 0;
                q->info.si_code = SI_USER;
                .

                break;
```

```
case (unsigned long) SEND_SIG_PRIV:
        clear_siginfo(&q->info);
        q->info.si_signo = sig;
        q->info.si_errno = 0;
        q->info.si_code = SI_KERNEL;

        .
        .

        .

        .

complete_signal(sig, t, type);
}
```

While retrieving the "sigpending" structure, if the signal is meant for that single thread, it uses the "pending" structure in the "task_struct". Otherwise it uses the "shared_pending" structure of the "signal" structure in "task_struct". Next, a "sigqueue" structure is allocated and added to the tail of retrieved "sigpending" structure. The "kernel_siginfo" structure info is updated accordingly.

There are a lot of other things that this function does, like handling a condition when the "sigqueue" cannot be allocated, some extra processing for signals delivered to groups, etc. But we will not delve into those details here.
The function "complete_signal()" is called in the end.

The execution path which starts from the function "complete_signal()" takes care of waking up the process (if required) so that the signal can be processed.
It sets the "TIF_SIGPENDING" flag through the function sequence "complete_signal() -> signal_wake_up() -> signal_wake_up_state()". This flag indicates that there is a signal pending. It will be discussed later when we talk about signal handling.
After that, it uses the function "kick_process()" to make the process enter kernel mode, so that the signal can be handled.

Signal Handling

Signal handling is performed when a process is returning from the kernel mode to the user mode. This is the case when a system call has finished execution. The function "do_syscall_64()" executes a system call, and in the end calls "syscall_return_slowpath()", which in turn calls the function "prepare_exit_to_usermode()".

The function "prepare_exit_to_usermode()" performs the first check for any pending signals.

```
__visible inline void prepare_exit_to_usermode(struct
pt_regs *regs)
{
      .
      .

    if (unlikely(cached_flags &
EXIT_TO_USERMODE_LOOP_FLAGS))
               exit_to_usermode_loop(regs, cached_flags);

      .
      .
}
```

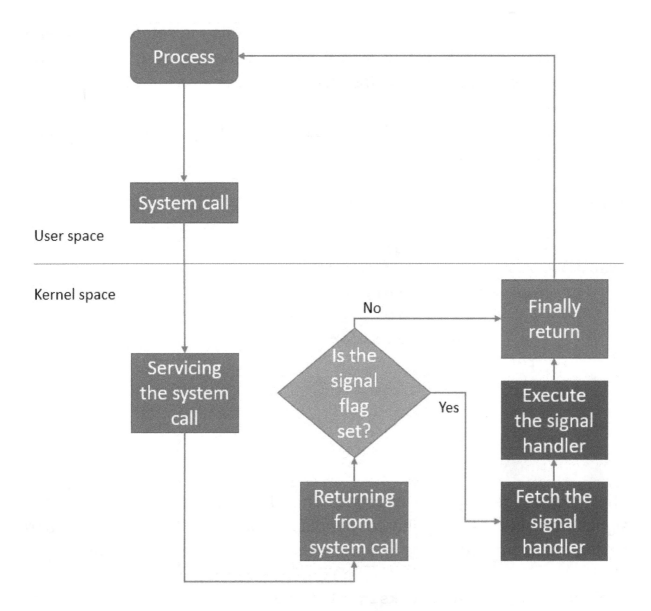

The above diagram depicts a high-level view of when the signal handler is invoked.

The EXIT_TO_USERMODE_LOOP_FLAGS macro in the above code, among other things, is being used to check if there is a signal pending or not. In case there is, the function "exit_to_usermode_loop()" is called.

The function "exit_to_usermode_loop()" performs specific checks for each flag. It also checks for the signal flag TIF_SIGPENDING, through the macro _TIF_SIGPENDING. If you recall, the flag TIF_SIGPENDING was set when a signal was delivered to a process. In case the flag is set, it would mean that there is a pending signal, and it needs to be handled. The function "do_signal()" is called to handle the signal.

The function "do_signal()" first retrieves the pending signal from the data structures, and delivers it.

```
void do_signal(struct pt_regs *regs)
{
    struct ksignal ksig;

    if (get_signal(&ksig)) {
        /* Whee! Actually deliver the signal.  */
            handle_signal(&ksig, regs);
        return;
    }
    .
    .
    .

}
```

The function "get_signal()" is called. This does the job of dequeuing the signal from the pending/shared_pending structures of the process and setting the appropriate fields in "ksig" with the dequeued signal data.

```
bool get_signal(struct ksignal *ksig)
{
    struct sighand_struct *sighand = current->sighand;
    struct signal_struct *signal = current->signal;
    int signr;
    .
    .

    try_to_freeze();
    .
    .

    for (;;) {
        struct k_sigaction *ka;
        .
```

```
         .
    signr = dequeue_synchronous_signal(&ksig->info);
    if (!signr)
                    signr = dequeue_signal(current,
&current->blocked, &ksig->info);

         .

         .

    ka = &sighand->action[signr-1];

         .

         .

    if (ka->sa.sa_handler != SIG_DFL) {
              /* Run the handler.  */
              ksig->ka = *ka;

         .

}

         .

    ksig->sig = signr;
    return ksig->sig > 0;
}
```

The function "get_signal()" first tries to freeze the process through the function "try_to_freeze()". This is used to check whether the kernel has instructed the processes to go for a freeze. This is done when the system is going for hibernation. The kernel sets a flag, and then sends a fake signal to all user-space threads, which leads them to this part of the code.

Next it goes into a loop and tries to dequeue the signals. It does this for synchronous signals first, by calling the function "dequeue_synchronous_signal()". The function "dequeue_synchronous_signal()" takes each entry from the "pending" structure of task_struct" and checks whether they are synchronous signals or not. The first synchronous signal found is deleted from the "pending" structure and returned. The "ksig->info" structure is also updated with the relevant data of the signal returned.

If there are no synchronous signals to be handled, the function "get_signal()" calls the function "dequeue_signal()" to check if there are any asynchronous signals available to be handled. The "dequeue_signal()" function first checks the "pending" structure of "task_struct" for any available signal, and then checks "shared_pending" structure of "task_struct->signal". This is done through the function "__dequeue_signal()".

```
int dequeue_signal(struct task_struct *tsk, sigset_t *mask,
kernel_siginfo_t *info)
{
    .

    .

    signr = __dequeue_signal(&tsk->pending, mask, info,
&resched_timer);
        if (!signr) {
        signr = __dequeue_signal(&tsk->signal->shared_pending,
                    mask, info, &resched_timer);

    .

}
```

The function "__dequeue_signal()" first calls "next_signal() for quickly checking if there is a signal to be handled, and then calls "collect_signal()" to dequeue the "sigqueue" structure from the list and update the "info" fields with the dequeued signal. This "info" is actually the "ksig->info" structure sent by the function "get_signal()" above.

Next, in the "get_signal()", the dequeued signal "k_sigaction" structure is extracted from the "sighand" structure using the returned signal number "signr".

```
ka = &sighand->action[signr-1];
```

Recall that the "k_sigaction" structure holds the "sigaction" structure which contains the "sa_handler" field, which is the handle to the task to be performed for that particular signal.

Now, the "ksig" structure is updated with the handler of the extracted signal.

```
if (ka->sa.sa_handler != SIG_DFL) {
        /* Run the handler.  */
        ksig->ka = *ka;
```

Now let us go back to our main function "do_signal()".

```
void do_signal(struct pt_regs *regs)
{
    struct ksignal ksig;

    if (get_signal(&ksig)) {
        /* Whee! Actually deliver the signal.  */
            handle_signal(&ksig, regs);
        return;
    }
    .
    .
    .
}
```

The signal has been dequeued and updated in the "ksig" structure. The function "handle_signal()" is called next. This function will change the course of execution for the running process and make it execute the signal handler for the dequeued signal.

The function "handle_signal()" calls "setup_rt_frame()", which in turn calls "__setup_rt_frame()".

The function "__setup_rt_frame()" sets up the registers to execute the signal handler. If we peek into the function, we can see that the instruction pointer of the program is getting updated to the signal handler.

```
static int __setup_rt_frame(int sig, struct ksignal *ksig,
                sigset_t *set, struct pt_regs *regs)
{
    .
    frame = get_sigframe(&ksig->ka, regs, sizeof(struct
rt_sigframe), &fp);
    .
    regs->si = (unsigned long)&frame->info;
    regs->dx = (unsigned long)&frame->uc;
    regs->ip = (unsigned long) ksig->ka.sa.sa_handler;
    .
```

```
}
```

If something goes haywire while setting up the frame, the function "handling_signal()" sends a SIGSEGV signal to the process, through the function "signal_setup_done()".

Signal Overloading in User Space

In this section we will look at an example of changing the action a process takes when a particular signal is sent to it. A new handler for signal can be written, and signal handling can be changed accordingly from the user space. This is done using the system call "sigaction()". Before delving into the kernel code flow related to how this is done, let us see a simple user space C program which overrides SIGINT.

```c
#include<signal.h>
#include<stdio.h>

/* Handler function */
void handler(int sig) {
        printf("Receive signal: %u\n", sig);
};

int main(void) {
        struct sigaction sig_a;

        /* Initialize the signal handler structure */
        sig_a.sa_handler = handler;
        sigemptyset(&sig_a.sa_mask);
        sig_a.sa_flags = 0;

        /* Assign a new handler function to the SIGINT
signal */
        sigaction(SIGINT, &sig_a, NULL);
```

```
        /* Block and wait until a signal arrives */
        while (1) {
                sigsuspend(&sig_a.sa_mask);
                printf("loop\n");
        }
        return 0;
};
```

This code assigns a new handler for SIGINT signal, namely the function "handler()". This function, when invoked will only print a simple message and exit. This way we will know that a signal was sent to this process and our custom handler is being called.

SIGINT can be sent to the running process using Ctrl+C key combination. It is also equivalent to the bash command "kill -2 <pid>" where <pid> would be the pid of the above running program.

Also following key combination can be used to send specific signals :

CTRL-C - sends **SIGINT** whose default action is to terminate the application.

CTRL-\ - sends **SIGQUIT** whose default action is to terminate the application dumping core.

CTRL-Z - sends **SIGSTOP** which suspends the program.

If you compile and run the above C program then you will get the following O/P

```
[root@linux signal]# ./a.out
Receive signal: 2
loop
Receive signal: 2
loop
^CReceive signal: 2
loop
```

Even with **Ctrl+C** or **kill -2 \<pid\>** the process will not terminate, since we have changed the handler for that signal (SIGINT). Instead it will execute our custom signal handler and return.

If we look at the implementation of the system call "sigaction", we will observe that it updates the "k_sigaction" field of the "sighand" structure of "task_struct".

```
SYSCALL_DEFINE3(sigaction, int, sig, const struct sigaction
__user *, act,
    struct sigaction __user *, oact)
{
    .
    ret = do_sigaction(sig, act ? &new_ka : NULL, oact ?
&old_ka : NULL);
    .
}


int do_sigaction(int sig, struct k_sigaction *act, struct
k_sigaction *oact)
{
    .
    k = &p->sighand->action[sig-1];
    .
    if (act) {
        sigdelsetmask(&act->sa.sa_mask,
                    sigmask(SIGKILL) |
sigmask(SIGSTOP));
        *k = *act;
        .
    }
    .
}
```

System calls and signals

"Slow" syscalls, e.g. blocking read/write, put processes into a waiting state: TASK_INTERRUPTIBLE or TASK_UNINTERRUPTIBLE.

A task in state TASK_INTERRUPTIBLE will be changed to the TASK_RUNNING state by a signal. TASK_RUNNING state of a process means the process can be scheduled. If executed, its signal handler will be run before completion of "slow" syscall. The syscall does not complete by default.

If the SA_RESTART flag is set, syscall is restarted after the signal handler finishes.

Chapter 7   Kernel Synchronization

What is synchronization, and why is it needed?

Think of a system running multiple processes concurrently. If multiple processes have the need to access/change a single data resource, and they end up doing so together, it might result in data corruption or reading of incorrect data value. This kind of problem requires the use of some sort of synchronization.

In the above example, if the processes running in parallel are not coerced into accessing the data resource in a particular way, it might lead to a race condition, in which the result of execution is dependent on the timing of context switches of processes, which will lead to problems.

Synchronization primitives provide a way of forcing the access of critical resources in a mutually exclusive manner. This ensures that no two processes access/change the data resource at the same time.

It also helps with other issues that arise with concurrent execution of processes, i.e. deadlock, starvation, etc. A detailed discussion of these topics is out of scope of this book.

An atomic variable

In a multiprocessor system, there are cases when resources are being shared between processes. In such a scenario, modification (addition/subtraction) of a resource by more than one process can lead to a race condition, which can result in erroneous results. For such scenarios, the Linux kernel has "atomic_t" structures. These structures provide a way to atomically modify values of a variable, which prevents race conditions.

Global definition :

```
typedef struct {
        int counter;
} atomic_t;
```

```
#ifdef CONFIG_64BIT
typedef struct {
        long counter;
} atomic64_t;
#endif
```

These variables are wrapped in a struct so that casting into normal integer types is not allowed.

Difference between atomic_set(v, i) and v = value

Speaking in terms of what each of them do, there is no difference. Both the above assign the "value" to v. But how they do it differs, because the assignment operation "atomic_set()" for atomic variables needs to take care of a number of problems which might arise due to compiler optimization.

Let us talk about the compiler optimizations which lead to problems. The first problem is Load/Store tearing, in which a multi byte load store instruction might get broken down by the compiler to process a single byte at a time, which leaves the single instruction non-atomic. The second is more direct. C compilers nowadays do not guarantee that a word access would be atomic. So, we need some way of instructing the compiler to avoid the above optimizations. Enter "volatile" variables.

When we look at the code of "atomic_set()", we see that it calls the macro "WRITE_ONCE", which ultimately calls the generic inline function "__write_once_size()".
The "__write_once_size()" function uses the volatile keyword to command the compiler to skip optimizations (mentioned above) on the statements.

```
static __always_inline void __write_once_size(volatile void
*p, void *res, int size)
{
    switch (size) {
```

```
case 1: *(volatile __u8 *)p = *(__u8 *)res; break;
case 2: *(volatile __u16 *)p = *(__u16 *)res; break;
case 4: *(volatile __u32 *)p = *(__u32 *)res; break;
case 8: *(volatile __u64 *)p = *(__u64 *)res; break;
default:
barrier();
__builtin_memcpy((void *)p, (const void *)res, size);
barrier();
  }
}
```

Difference between atomic_add and v = v + i

When we look at the way "atomic_add()" works, and internally what it does, we realize that there is a difference between "atomic_add()" and "v = v + i;" in what they do (unlike atomic_set).

"atomic_add()" calls the function "atomic_add_return()" which calls two functions, namely "kasan_check_write()" and "arch_atomic_add_return". The first function is part of the kernel address sanitizer (kasan), which detects and reports memory errors such as use-after-free and out-of-bound bugs. We will not be discussing the internal working of kasan in this book.

The second function is "arch_atomic_add_return()". This function calls the function "xadd()" which ultimately lands in the function "__xchg_op()" after a number of calls. The "xadd()" function also adds another parameter to this calling sequence, "LOCK_PREFIX".

When we look at the internal code of "__xchg_op()" we see two things. Firstly it executes the instruction with the "LOCK_PREFIX" sent to it, and secondly that it executes the "xadd" instruction on the parameters. We will look into both of these steps one by one.

The LOCK_PREFIX is the key to making the multiple instructions atomic.. In this way the CPU cannot be preempted before the operation takes effect.

It prevents processors from writing to the same memory location at the same time. This ensures that the processor has exclusive use of any shared memory. This makes sure that the 3 steps (READ, MODIFY and WRITE) appears as a single step to other processors.

In older generation architectures, the LOCK_PREFIX was executed by asserting a lock on the bus, which came with a big hit in performance. But with newer architectures, the lock is asserted on the cache line. This change, along with the cache coherency protocol, ensures that the access to the shared memory is managed.

The name xadd stands for exchange and add. This instruction exchanges the values of the destination and the source operand and stores the sum of the two in the destination operand. The exchange is done to make sure that after the destination is updated with the sum of the values, the original value of the destination is still retained in the source operand. This was a desired feature before xadd was added to the instruction set.

```
#define xadd(ptr, inc)          __xadd((ptr), (inc),
LOCK_PREFIX)

#define __xadd(ptr, inc, lock)  __xchg_op((ptr), (inc),
xadd, lock)

#define __xchg_op(ptr, arg, op, lock)                    \
    ({                                                   \
            __typeof__ (*(ptr)) __ret = (arg);           \
        switch (sizeof(*(ptr))) {                        \
        case __X86_CASE_B:                               \
            asm volatile (lock #op "b %b0, %1\n"         \
                    : "+q" (__ret), "+m" (*(ptr))        \
                    : : "memory", "cc");                 \
        Break;
```

Spinlock

Spinlock structure

Lets look into the contents of the main "spinlock" structure.

```
typedef struct spinlock {
    union {
    struct raw_spinlock rlock;

#ifdef CONFIG_DEBUG_LOCK_ALLOC
# define LOCK_PADSIZE (offsetof(struct raw_spinlock,
dep_map))
    struct {
        u8 __padding[LOCK_PADSIZE];
        struct lockdep_map dep_map;
    };
#endif
    };
} spinlock_t;
```

Ignoring the DEBUG portion, we take a dive into the "raw_spinlock" member.

```
typedef struct raw_spinlock {
    arch_spinlock_t raw_lock;
#ifdef CONFIG_DEBUG_SPINLOCK
    unsigned int magic, owner_cpu;
    void *owner;
#endif
#ifdef CONFIG_DEBUG_LOCK_ALLOC
    struct lockdep_map dep_map;
#endif
} raw_spinlock_t;
```

Again, ignoring the DEBUG portion, we can see that the main member of this structure is "raw_lock".

We've come to the main structure which controls the working of spinlocks (arch_spinlock_t). It is worth knowing that the spinlock implementation in kernel 5.0 uses queues. So, we look into the implementation of the queued spinlocks (qspinlock).

Older spinlocks used something called ticketing, but we will not be discussing that here. We will discuss how queues are used to make the threads trying to acquire the spinlock wait in a fair manner in the later section when we discuss acquiring a spinlock.

```
typedef struct qspinlock {
    union {
        atomic_t val;

        /*
         * By using the whole 2nd least significant byte
for the
         * pending bit, we can allow better optimization of
the lock
         * acquisition for the pending bit holder.
         */
#ifdef __LITTLE_ENDIAN
        struct {
            u8  locked;
            u8  pending;
        };
        struct {
            u16 locked_pending;
            u16 tail;
        };
#else
        struct {
            u16 tail;
            u16 locked_pending;
        };
        struct {
            u8  reserved[2];
            u8  pending;
            u8  locked;
```

```
        };
#endif
    };
} arch_spinlock_t;
```

Looking into the "qspinlock" structure above, we see that it just contains one union. The member "val", which is of atomic_t type, is used to read/write data. This data is divided into relevant groups of bits. The first 8 bits are used to denote whether the spinlock is locked or not. Bit 8 is used as a pending bit. The usage of this bit will be explained when we discuss how the spinlock is acquired in later sections. Rest of the bits are used for storing the tail of the queue (some bits are not used for certain configurations).

Initialization of spinlock

"spin_lock_init()" function is used to initialize a spinlock.
The main function which "spin_lock_init()" calls is "raw_spin_lock_init()". The calling sequence is "spin_lock_init() -> raw_spin_lock_init() -> __RAW_SPIN_LOCK_UNLOCKED() -> __RAW_SPIN_LOCK_INITIALIZER()".

```
#define spin_lock_init(_lock)                    \
do {                                             \
    spinlock_check(_lock);                       \
    raw_spin_lock_init(&(_lock)->rlock);         \
} while (0)

# define raw_spin_lock_init(lock)                \
    do { *(lock) = __RAW_SPIN_LOCK_UNLOCKED(lock); } while
(0)

#define __RAW_SPIN_LOCK_UNLOCKED(lockname)   \
    (raw_spinlock_t) __RAW_SPIN_LOCK_INITIALIZER(lockname)

#define __RAW_SPIN_LOCK_INITIALIZER(lockname)    \
    {                                            \
```

```
      .raw_lock = __ARCH_SPIN_LOCK_UNLOCKED,  \
    SPIN_DEBUG_INIT(lockname)            \
    SPIN_DEP_MAP_INIT(lockname)  }
```

```
#define __ARCH_SPIN_LOCK_UNLOCKED   { { 0 } }
```

"__RAW_SPIN_LOCK_INITIALIZER()" sets the raw_lock member of the spinlock struct to 0. This initializes the spinlock and sets its state to unlocked.

Acquiring a spinlock

For acquiring a spinlock, there are multiple functions. Each function has the main task of trying to acquire the spinlock, plus some extra tasks. We will see each function in detail and try to find out how they work.

spin_lock() function

The simple calling sequence of the function is "spin_lock() -> raw_spin_lock() -> _raw_spin_lock() -> __raw_spin_lock()".
__raw_spin_lock() contains 3 macros.

```
static inline void __raw_spin_lock(raw_spinlock_t *lock)
{
    preempt_disable();
    spin_acquire(&lock->dep_map, 0, 0, _RET_IP_);
    LOCK_CONTENDED(lock, do_raw_spin_trylock,
do_raw_spin_lock);
}
```

The function "preempt_disable()" does exactly what its name says. It disables preemption so that the scheduler cannot preempt the thread while it is spinning and waiting on this lock. This is needed because we don't want the scheduler to preempt the running thread while it is spinning on the spinlock. Older kernels used a variable in the thread structure to control preemption. Newer ones have moved to a per-cpu variable for controlling preemption, since accessing per-cpu variables is cheaper than accessing the variable from the thread structure.

```
#define preempt_disable() \
do { \
    preempt_count_inc(); \
    barrier(); \
} while (0)

#define preempt_count_inc() preempt_count_add(1)

void preempt_count_add(int val)
{
.

.

    __preempt_count_add(val);

.

.

}
```

This per-cpu variable named "__preempt_count" is incremented; and when the scheduler sees that this variable is incremented (function "preempt_schedule()") it returns without preempting the thread.

```
static __always_inline void __preempt_count_add(int val)
{
    raw_cpu_add_4(__preempt_count, val);
}
```

"spin_acquire()" is a macro which calls "lock_acquire_exclusive()" with the relevant parameters. "lock_acquire_exclusive()" calls "lock_acquire()" which then calls "__lock_acquire()". To understand the workings of this function we must deep dive into the kernels lockdep design and architecture. Lockdep's main job is to try to detect a deadlock (or a potential deadlock) that can occur due to locking operations. It does this by creating dependency graphs between locks as and when they are acquired and released. We will not go into the details of the architecture and workings of lockdep here.

"LOCK_CONTENDED()" is the main macro which does the job of waiting on the spinlock if it is not available. The calling sequence is "LOCK_CONTENDED() -> do_raw_spin_lock() -> arch_spin_lock() -> queued_spin_lock()". The function "queued_spin_lock()" starts with the fastpath through the function "atomic_try_cmpxchg_acquire()", in which it just checks whether the lock is free or not. If the lock is free, it acquires the lock and returns.

```
static __always_inline void queued_spin_lock(struct
qspinlock *lock)
{
    u32 val = 0;

    if (likely(atomic_try_cmpxchg_acquire(&lock->val, &val,
_Q_LOCKED_VAL)))
        return;

    queued_spin_lock_slowpath(lock, val);
}
```

If the lock is not free, the slowpath is taken and the function "queued_spin_lock_slowpath()" is called. The code from this function is too big to be posted here, so we only go through different stages of locking and waiting. The slowpath uses a pending bit and an mcs spinlock structure (for building the queue). Let us try to understand the working of the slowpath using a scenario in which different threads (running on different CPUs) try to acquire a spinlock one by one. When CPU-1 (running the first thread) comes along to acquire the lock, it is free; hence the first CPU acquires the lock. This is the fastpath which we discussed a little earlier. cpu 2 comes along and sees that the lock is acquired, but there is no one else waiting for this lock since the pending bit is not set. CPU-2 just sets the pending bit and waits; this is the pending state. When cpu 3 comes to acquire the lock, it sees that the pending bit is set, which means the lock is acquired and there is another CPU waiting for the lock. CPU-3 then starts building the queue of mcs spinlock structure; this is the uncontended queue state. In case a CPU-4 comes and sees that the pending bit is set, and there is also a queue waiting, it adds itself to the queue; this is the contended queue state. When the lock is released, the CPUs acquire the lock one by one on an FCFS basis. For acquiring the lock, they set the "locked" member variable in their qspinlock structure to 1. This member variable is used later while releasing the lock.

spin_lock_bh() function

This function performs all the tasks performed by the "spin_lock()" function above, in addition, it disables the software interrupts for the calling thread.

The function calling sequence is "spin_lock_bh() -> raw_spin_lock_bh(lock) -> _raw_spin_lock_bh() -> __raw_spin_lock_bh()".

"__raw_spin_lock_bh()" calls "__local_bh_disable_ip()", "spin_acquire()" and "LOCK_CONTENDED()". We will only discuss "__local_bh_disable_ip()" since the remaining functions have already been explained in the previous section.

```
static inline void __raw_spin_lock_bh(raw_spinlock_t *lock)
{
    __local_bh_disable_ip(_RET_IP_, SOFTIRQ_LOCK_OFFSET);
    spin_acquire(&lock->dep_map, 0, 0, _RET_IP_);
    LOCK_CONTENDED(lock, do_raw_spin_trylock,
do_raw_spin_lock);
}
```

"__local_bh_disable_ip()" is called with the macro SOFTIRQ_LOCK_OFFSET. We notice that "__local_bh_disable_ip()" goes and increments the same per-cpu "__preempt_count" variable which was incremented while disabling preemption. This is oksy, because the macro

SOFTIRQ_LOCK_OFFSET controls which bits are to be modified while incrementing __preempt_count.

```
void __local_bh_disable_ip(unsigned long ip, unsigned int cnt)
{
.

__preempt_count_add(cnt);

.

}
```

If we look around a little, we discover that the variable "__preempt_count" is used for multiple purposes, including preemption, software interrupts, hardware interrupts and others. Bits 0-7 are used for preemption, 8-15 are used for software interrupts, 16-23 are used for hardware interrupts, and so on. So, SOFTIRQ_LOCK_OFFSET will disable preemption and software interrupts.

spin_lock_irq() function
This function performs all the tasks performed by the "spin_lock()" function above, in addition disables the hardware interrupts (excluding the non-maskable ones) for the calling thread.
The function calling sequence is "spin_lock_irq() -> raw_spin_lock_irq(lock) -> _raw_spin_lock_irq() -> __raw_spin_lock_irq()".

"__raw_spin_lock_irq()" calls four functions (see below). Among them the new one is "local_irq_disable()". Others have been discussed before.

local_irq_disable()'s calling sequence is "local_irq_disable() -> raw_local_irq_disable() -> arch_local_irq_disable() -> native_irq_disable()", which executes the "CLI" instruction.

```
static inline void native_irq_disable(void)
{
    asm volatile("cli": : :"memory");
}
```

This instruction clears the interrupt enable bit, which makes the CPU ignore all the hardware interrupts (except the non-maskable ones).

Releasing a spinlock

For releasing a spinlock, there are multiple functions. Each function has the main task of trying to acquire the spinlock, plus some extra tasks. We will see each function in detail and try to find out how they work.

These functions correspond directly to the spinlock acquiring function discussed earlier. The extra tasks that were performed while acquiring, corresponds to the extra tasks that need to be done while releasing.

spin_unlock() function

This function corresponds to the "spin_lock()" function used for acquiring the lock. If releases the lock and performs other relevant tasks like

The function calling sequence is "spin_unlock() -> raw_spin_unlock() -> _raw_spin_unlock() -> __raw_spin_unlock()".

"__raw_spin_unlock()" calls "spin_realease()", "do_raw_spin_unlock()" and "preempt_enable()". Let us discuss them one by one.

"spin_release()" calls "lock_release()" which in turn calls "__lock_release()". "__lock_release()" takes care of the tasks related to lockdep, which tracks the lock dependencies in the kernel. We won't be delving into the internals of this function.

"do_raw_spin_unlock()" is the main function which takes care of releasing the lock. Its calling sequence is "arch_spin_unlock(l) -> queued_spin_unlock() -> smp_store_release()". When we look into the function "smp_store_release()" we see that it uses the WRITE_ONCE macro to update the "locked" member variable of the qspinlock structure. Notice that the "locked" variable is an atomic type variable, which we had discussed in one of the earlier sections in this chapter.

```
#define smp_store_release(p, v)        \
do {                                   \
    barrier();                  \
    WRITE_ONCE(*p, v);                 \
} while (0)
```

This signifies that the lock is not held anymore. The thread which was waiting for the lock on the pending bit acquires the lock. Remember, this was the thread which had tried to acquire the lock first; the others would be waiting in the queue.

"preempt_enable()" does the exact opposite of "preempt_disable()".

```
#define preempt_enable() \
do { \
    barrier(); \
    preempt_count_dec(); \
} while (0)

#define preempt_count_dec() preempt_count_sub(1)

void preempt_count_sub(int val)
{
    .
    __preempt_count_sub(val);
}

static __always_inline void __preempt_count_sub(int val)
{
    raw_cpu_add_4(__preempt_count, -val);
}
```

It enables preemption by decrementing the per-cpu variable "__preempt_count". With the value of "__preempt_count" back to normal, the scheduler can preempt the thread if needed.

spin_unlock_bh() function

This function is used to unlock the spinlock if it has been locked using "spin_lock_bh()".

The functions calling sequence is "spin_unlock_bh() -> raw_spin_unlock_bh(lock) -> _raw_spin_unlock_bh() -> __raw_spin_unlock_bh()".

"__raw_spin_unlock_bh()" calls "spin_release()", "do_raw_spin_unlock()" and "__local_bh_enable_ip()". We will only discuss "__local_bh_enable_ip()" since others have been discussed before.

"__local_bh_enable_ip()" is called with the macro SOFTIRQ_LOCK_OFFSET, which clearly indicates that it is going to enable preemption and software interrupts, by changing the appropriate bits in the per-cpu variable "__preempt_count".

```
void __local_bh_enable_ip(unsigned long ip, unsigned int cnt)
{
.

    preempt_count_sub(cnt - 1);


    preempt_count_dec();
.
    preempt_check_resched();
}
```

However, it does not enable both together. The function "__local_bh_enable_ip()" enables software interrupts first, and then checks if any software interrupts are pending (could have arrived while the thread was holding the spinlock). If there are any pending software interrupts, those are serviced first. Once that is done, then the preemption is enabled.

spin_unlock_irq() function

The functions calling sequence is "spin_unlock_irq() -> raw_spin_unlock_irq(lock) -> _raw_spin_unlock_irq() -> __raw_spin_unlock_irq()".

"__raw_spin_unlock_irq()" calls four functions (see below). Among them, the only new one is "local_irq_enable()"; others have been discussed before.

```
static inline void __raw_spin_unlock_irq(raw_spinlock_t
*lock)
{
    spin_release(&lock->dep_map, 1, _RET_IP_);
    do_raw_spin_unlock(lock);
    local_irq_enable();
    preempt_enable();
}
```

local_irq_enable()'s calling sequence is "local_irq_enable() -> raw_local_irq_enable() -> arch_local_irq_enable() -> native_irq_enable()".

```
static inline void native_irq_enable(void)
{
    asm volatile("sti": : :"memory");
}
```

The function "native_irq_enable()" executes the "STI" assembly instruction. This instruction sets the interrupt enable bit, which enables all the hardware interrupts for that CPU.

Semaphore

Semaphore structure

Let's look at the main semaphore structure used in the Linux kernel.

```
struct semaphore {
    raw_spinlock_t      lock;
    unsigned int        count;
    struct list_head    wait_list;
};
```

This structure has three member variables. The first one is a spinlock, which is used while accessing and changing the member "count". This makes sure that multiple threads that want to acquire the semaphore do not access or update the count variable at the same time.

The member variable count is used to denote whether the semaphore is free (count will be > 0), or acquired by some other thread (count will be <= 0).

The member variable "wait_list" is the linked list of all the threads that are waiting for this semaphore to become available.

Initialization of semaphore

To initialize a semaphore, the function "sema_init()" function is used.

```
static inline void sema_init(struct semaphore *sem, int val)
{
    static struct lock_class_key __key;
    *sem = (struct semaphore) __SEMAPHORE_INITIALIZER(*sem, val);
    lockdep_init_map(&sem->lock.dep_map, "semaphore->lock", &__key, 0);
}

#define DEFINE_SEMAPHORE(name)  \
```

```
    struct semaphore name = __SEMAPHORE_INITIALIZER(name,
1)
```

```
#define __SEMAPHORE_INITIALIZER(name, n)                    \
{                                              \
    .lock       = __RAW_SPIN_LOCK_UNLOCKED((name).lock),   \
    .count      = n,                            \
    .wait_list  = LIST_HEAD_INIT((name).wait_list),      \
}
```

The final macro "__SEMAPHORE_INITIALIZER" initializes the spinlock to an unlocked state. Next it sets "count" to the number passed to it. This denotes the number of parallel threads that can acquire the semaphore. The list is initialized to empty.

This function can be used multiple times on the semaphore to initialize it back to the values needed. However, a semaphore should not be initialized simultaneously by multiple threads, nor should it be initialized while it is in use by other threads.

How to take the lock

Acquiring the semaphore is performed using the down() function.

```
void down(struct semaphore *sem)
{
    unsigned long flags;

    raw_spin_lock_irqsave(&sem->lock, flags);
    if (likely(sem->count > 0))
        sem->count--;
    else
        __down(sem);
    raw_spin_unlock_irqrestore(&sem->lock, flags);
}
```

The function first checks the value of "count", since "count" denotes the number of threads that can acquire the semaphore. Theoretically, "count" can also denote the number of resources available, which the semaphore is protecting. If the number (sem->count) is greater than 0, then it simply decrements the "count" of that semaphore and returns.

If not, the "__down()" function is called, which calls

```
static noinline void __sched __down(struct semaphore *sem)
{
      __down_common(sem, TASK_UNINTERRUPTIBLE,
MAX_SCHEDULE_TIMEOUT);
}

static inline int __sched __down_common(struct semaphore
*sem, long state,
                                    long timeout)
{
    struct semaphore_waiter waiter;

    list_add_tail(&waiter.list, &sem->wait_list);
    .
    .

        __set_current_state(state);
    raw_spin_unlock_irq(&sem->lock);
    timeout = schedule_timeout(timeout);
    .
    .
    .
}
```

The function "__down"common()" takes the current thread which has requested for the semaphore access (by calling down), and adds it to the "wait_list" of that semaphore. To add the thread to the wait_list, the structure "semaphore_waiter" is used. This structure stores the "task_struct" structure of the current thread. This will be used later to wake up this thread.

```
struct semaphore_waiter {
    struct list_head list;
    struct task_struct *task;
    bool up;
};
```

So essentially now the semaphore knows that this thread wants to acquire it, and is now waiting since the count was <= 0. This will be used when another process calls the "up()" function on this semaphore, as we will see in a while.

It is also important to note that once the thread is in the "wait_list" of the semaphore, it goes into the "TASK_UNINTERRUPTIBLE" state.
There is also a timeout involved, which dictates for how long this process is going to wait for the semaphore to become available.

How to release the lock

When a semaphore is to be released, "up()" function is called

```
void up(struct semaphore *sem)
{
    unsigned long flags;

    raw_spin_lock_irqsave(&sem->lock, flags);
    if (likely(list_empty(&sem->wait_list)))
        sem->count++;
    else
        __up(sem);
    raw_spin_unlock_irqrestore(&sem->lock, flags);
}
```

The "up()" function performs the check if the "wait_list" of the semaphore is empty or not. This is the same list where a thread would have got added when a "down()" was called on the semaphore and the count was <= 0.

If the "wait_list" is empty, then the "up()" function just increments "count" and returns.

If the "wait_list" is not empty, it calls the "__up()" function. This is done to signal one of the waiting threads to wake up.

```
static noinline void __sched __up(struct semaphore *sem)
{
    struct semaphore_waiter *waiter =
list_first_entry(&sem->wait_list,
                    struct semaphore_waiter, list);
    list_del(&waiter->list);
    waiter->up = true;
    wake_up_process(waiter->task);
}
```

The "__up()" function extracts the first entry in the "wait_list" of the semaphore. Remember that this entry is of type "semaphore_waiter", which holds a pointer to the "task_struct" of the waiting thread. This reference to the "task_struct" of the waiting thread is passed on to the function "wake_up_process()"

Traversing through this function call sequence, the "wake_up_process()" function would fall into the scheduler code. Using the "enqueue_task" function pointer, the thread is handed over to the configured scheduler (function "activate_task()"). The thread state is also changed to "TASK_RUNNING" through the function "ttwu_do_wakeup()".

Mutex

Mutex structure

```
struct mutex {
    atomic_long_t       owner;
    spinlock_t      wait_lock;
#ifdef CONFIG_MUTEX_SPIN_ON_OWNER
```

```
        struct optimistic_spin_queue osq; /* Spinner MCS lock
*/
#endif
    struct list_head   wait_list;
#ifdef CONFIG_DEBUG_MUTEXES
    void            *magic;
#endif
#ifdef CONFIG_DEBUG_LOCK_ALLOC
    struct lockdep_map  dep_map;
#endif
};
```

Ignoring the DEBUG portions, the structure has three main members. The members "wait_lock" and "wait_list" serve the same purpose as they did in the semaphore structure described before. The member variable "owner" of the mutex structure holds information about the current owner of the mutex.

Initialization of mutex

To initialize a mutex, the macro "mutex_init()" is used.

```
#define mutex_init(mutex)                           \
do {                                        \
    static struct lock_class_key __key;         \
                                    \
    __mutex_init((mutex), #mutex, &__key);              \
} while (0)

__mutex_init(struct mutex *lock, const char *name, struct
lock_class_key *key)
{
    atomic_long_set(&lock->owner, 0);
    spin_lock_init(&lock->wait_lock);
    INIT_LIST_HEAD(&lock->wait_list);
#ifdef CONFIG_MUTEX_SPIN_ON_OWNER
    osq_lock_init(&lock->osq);
#endif
```

```
    debug_mutex_init(lock, name, key);
}
```

The final function "__mutex_init()" uses "spin_lock_init()" to initialize the spinlock "wait_lock". It initializes the "wait_list" to empty. The "owner" field is set to zero, which represents that the mutex is not held by anyone.

How to acquire a mutex

Acquiring a mutex lock is performed using the "mutex_lock()" function.

```
void __sched mutex_lock(struct mutex *lock)
{
    might_sleep();

    if (!__mutex_trylock_fast(lock))
        __mutex_lock_slowpath(lock);
}
```

Just like spinlock, the process of acquiring a mutex also has a fastpath and a slowpath. If the mutex is free, then the fastpath succeeds; and the mutex gets acquired by the thread which called the "mutex_lock()" function.

```
static __always_inline bool __mutex_trylock_fast(struct mutex *lock)
{
    unsigned long curr = (unsigned long)current;
    unsigned long zero = 0UL;

    if (atomic_long_try_cmpxchg_acquire(&lock->owner, &zero, curr))
        return true;

    return false;
}
```

The fastpath just performs a simple compare and exchange instruction to achieve the above-mentioned task. If the mutex is already acquired by some other thread, then the execution falls into the slowpath.

Let us take a dive into the slowpath. Since the slowpath function is quite big, only certain relevant portions of the code will be displayed here. The reader is encouraged to look into the complete function for a clearer picture.

The slowpath function calling sequence is **__mutex_lock_slowpath() -> __mutex_lock() -> __mutex_lock_common()**

```
static int __sched
__mutex_lock(struct mutex *lock, long state, unsigned int subclass,
            struct lockdep_map *nest_lock, unsigned long ip)
{
    return __mutex_lock_common(lock, state, subclass,
nest_lock, ip, NULL, false);
}
```

Notice that in the function call to "__mutex_lock_common()", the second last parameter is "NULL", and the last one is "false". These correspond to the parameters "ww_ctx" and "use_ww_ctx" as shown below. These are used for a new feature in mutexes called wait and wound. Wait and wound mutexes have been introduced to tackle the possibility of a deadlock in a situation where two threads are holding two different resources, and each thread is waiting for the other one. In a "wait and wound" mutex, one thread has the power to make the other thread release their resource. This ensures that at least one of the threads can finish their processing. The other thread must start over from the beginning and try to acquire the first resource. We will not be delving into the code for "wait and wound" mutex here.

```
static __always_inline int __sched
__mutex_lock_common(struct mutex *lock, long state,
unsigned int subclass,
```

```
        struct lockdep_map *nest_lock, unsigned long ip,
        struct ww_acquire_ctx *ww_ctx, const bool
use_ww_ctx)
{
.

.
```

The slowpath for acquiring a mutex has two phases. First one is "optimistic spinning", in which the thread tries to wait for a little while for the mutex to get released. In this path the function first gets the owner who is currently holding the lock on the mutex and waits for it to release the lock. The function will come out of this optimistic spinning in one of the two cases. If the owner releases the lock, or if the owner sleeps or changes.
If that is successful, the lock is acquired and the code returns.

```
    if (__mutex_trylock(lock) ||
        mutex_optimistic_spin(lock, ww_ctx, use_ww_ctx,
NULL)) {
    /* got the lock, yay! */
    lock_acquired(&lock->dep_map, ip);
    if (use_ww_ctx && ww_ctx)
        ww_mutex_set_context_fastpath(ww, ww_ctx);
    preempt_enable();
    return 0;
    }
```

If the mutex is still not released after the "optimistic spinning", then the thread adds itself to the list of waiters (of the mutex lock), sets its state to "TASK_UNINTERRUPTIBLE", and calls the scheduler to preempt out.

```
if (!use_ww_ctx) {
    /* add waiting tasks to the end of the waitqueue
(FIFO): */
        __mutex_add_waiter(lock, &waiter, &lock-
>wait_list);
.

.
```

```
set_current_state(state);
for (;;) {
    .
    .
    .
schedule_preempt_disabled();
```

Notice that the thread is added to the "wait_list" only if the parameter "use_ww_ctx" is false.

Once the thread is scheduled out, it will be in the "TASK_UNINTERRUPTIBLE" state, until it is woken up. That is done when the mutex is released. We will see the details of this when we discuss the "mutex_unlock" function.

Assuming that the mutex was released by the thread which was holding it, this thread is woken up. The mutex is acquired through the function "__mutex_trylock()", and the thread is put into the "TASK_RUNNING" state. This is followed up by some basic cleaning like enabling preemption, unlocking the spinlock "wait_lock".

How to release a mutex

To release a semaphore, the function "mutex_unlock()" is used.

```
void __sched mutex_unlock(struct mutex *lock)
{
#ifndef CONFIG_DEBUG_LOCK_ALLOC
    if (__mutex_unlock_fast(lock))
    return;
#endif
    __mutex_unlock_slowpath(lock, _RET_IP_);
}
```

Here again we can observe that the code has two paths. The fast path quickly checks if there are any waiting processes for this mutex. If there are no waiting processes, then the "lock->owner" field is updated with all 0 bits, and the function "mutex_unlock()" returns.

However, there are processes waiting for this mutex, then the slowpath is triggered. The main job of slowpath here is to check the waiting processes, fetch the first entry from the "wait_list" and wake that task up.

```
static noinline void __sched __mutex_unlock_slowpath(struct
mutex *lock, unsigned long ip)
{
    .
    .

    owner = atomic_long_read(&lock->owner);
    .

    for (;;) {
    unsigned long old;
        .

        old  =  atomic_long_cmpxchg_release(&lock->owner,
owner,
                        __owner_flags(owner));
        if (old == owner) {
            if (owner & MUTEX_FLAG_WAITERS)
                Break;

        .

        .

        if (!list_empty(&lock->wait_list)) {
        /* get the first entry from the wait-list: */
        struct mutex_waiter *waiter =
            list_first_entry(&lock->wait_list,
                    struct mutex_waiter, list);
            .

        wake_q_add(&wake_q, next);
        }
        .

        wake_up_q(&wake_q);
}
```

You can observe that the first entry from the "wait_list" is being extracted. The waking up of the task is handled by the combination of "wake_q_add()" and "wake_up_q()" functions. The first one puts the task in a "wake_q_head" structure, and the second one extracts that task and calls "wake_up_process()" on it.

Chapter 8　Linux Memory Allocations

In this chapter we will go through various Linux memory allocation ways. We will see how to use different types of memory allocators.

Allocators and the APIs

The buddy allocator

The most basic allocator of Linux is the buddy allocator. Buddy allocator makes contiguous free list pools of page(n) (2^n pages) sized memory, where n represents the order of the list, and tries to allocate from those pages. Each list can be seen as a list of equal sized physically contiguous areas. The following figure depicts the N lists of pages. Each list has an order number. Zeroth order means the memory per node is 2^0 pages.

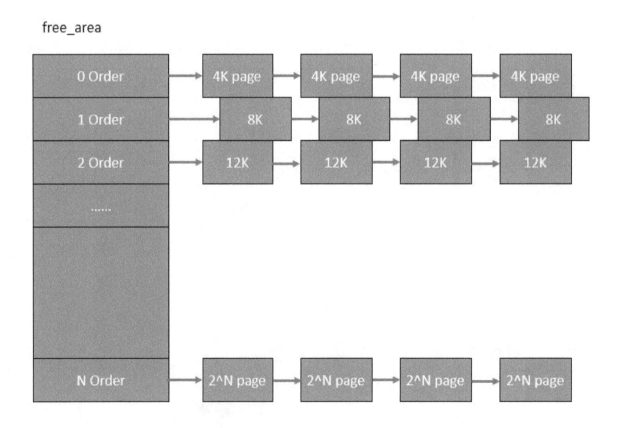

APIs based on this allocator are :

alloc_page/s

__get_free_page/s

These APIs allocate in multiples of pages.

The following diagram indicates the APIs and the allocator

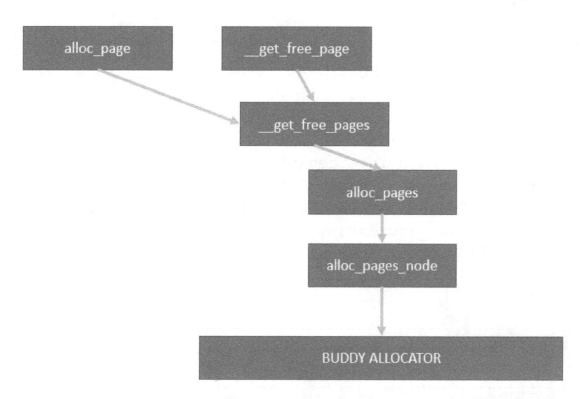

On a running system we can see the buddy info using cat /proc/buddyinfo :

```
root@x-vm:/home/x# cat /proc/buddyinfo
Node 0, zone      DMA      1      0      1      0      2
1      1      0      1      1      3
Node 0, zone      DMA32    2      2      1      1      1
2      2      2      4      4      744
Node 0, zone      Normal   3      618    953    350    260
172    69     13     27     7      2316
```

This shows that 11 orders are there from 0 to 10. It also shows the number of free entries per allocation.

Let us write a module to allocate using "alloc_pages()" and trace its function graph using ftrace.

```c
#include<linux/module.h>
#include<linux/version.h>
#include<linux/kernel.h>
#include<linux/init.h>
#include<linux/gfp.h>
#include<linux/mm.h>
struct page *my_alloc = NULL;
int myinit(void)
{
        unsigned long addr;
        printk("module inserted\n");
        my_alloc = alloc_pages(GFP_KERNEL, 1);
        printk("page address = 0x%08lx\n", my_alloc);
        addr = page_address(my_alloc);
        printk("virtual address = 0x%08lx\n", addr);
        return 0;
}

void myexit(void)
{
        if(my_alloc) {
                printk("module removed\n");
                __free_pages(my_alloc, 1);
        }
        printk("module removed\n");
}

module_init(myinit);
module_exit(myexit);
```

Tracing commands:

```
cd /sys/kernel/debug/tracing
cat /dev/null >  trace
echo alloc_pages_current > set_graph_function
echo 20 > max_graph_depth
echo function_graph > current_tracer
echo 1 > tracing_on
insmod /root/allocations/alloc_pages.ko
cp trace ~/alloc_pages_trace

echo 0 > tracing_on
echo > set_graph_function
echo 0 > max_graph_depth
cat /dev/null >  trace
rmmod alloc_pages
```

Trace :

```
2)                     |  alloc_pages_current() {
2)    0.186 us         |    get_task_policy.part.34();
2)    0.180 us         |    policy_nodemask();
2)    0.186 us         |    policy_node();
2)                     |    __alloc_pages_nodemask() {
2)                     |      _cond_resched() {
2)    0.184 us         |        rcu_all_qs();
2)    0.530 us         |      }
2)    0.178 us         |      should_fail_alloc_page();
2)                     |      get_page_from_freelist() {
2)    0.184 us         |        __inc_numa_state();
2)    0.185 us         |        __inc_numa_state();
2)    0.191 us         |        kernel_poison_pages();
2)    0.186 us         |        page_poisoning_enabled();
2)    2.206 us         |      }
2)    3.644 us         |    }
2)    5.114 us         |  }
```

Output in syslog :

```
Feb 26 20:38:54 x-vm kernel: [605189.840541] module
inserted
```

```
Feb 26 20:38:54 x-vm kernel: [605189.840550] page address =
0xffffea5c4d0a1580
Feb 26 20:38:54 x-vm kernel: [605189.840553] virtual
address = 0xffff8be082856000
Feb 26 20:39:12 x-vm kernel: [605208.014125] module removed
```

Resource map allocator

This is a different allocator which has fragmentation issues but is faster. This is also called a sequential fit allocator. This allocator allocates the first free block of any size from a chunk of memory.

APIs based on this allocator are :

vmalloc and family

This API is used to allocate a larger chunk of virtually contiguous area when we do not have it available. The physical area might not be contiguous.

"vmalloc()" allocates the virtual memory addresses between VMALLOC_START and VMALLOC_END.

Let's see the allocations for resource map allocator.
Say we get allocations and free requests in following sequence:

1. vmalloc(3000)
2. vmalloc(1000)
3. vfree(3000)
4. vmalloc(100)
5. vmalloc(2000)

Initial area has virtual addresses VMALLOC_START to VMALLOC_END

VMALLOC_START   VMALLOC_END

Alloc of 3000 bytes

3000 bytes	

Alloc of 1000 bytes

3000 bytes	1000 bytes	

Free of 3000 block

	1000 bytes	

Alloc of 100 bytes

100 bytes		1000 bytes	

Alloc of 2000 bytes

We can see that because of the use of resource map allocator, vmalloc suffers from internal fragmentation.

You will be surprised to know that vmalloc at the end uses "alloc_pages()" API itself. The scattered pages of RAM are made to point to contiguous virtual addresses using page table modifications.

Lets see the functions vmalloc calls:

"vmalloc()"
__vmalloc_node_range
__get_vm_area_node
      alloc_vmap_area
alloc_pages_current -- allocates page using buddy allocator
map_vm_area -- here we see that the init_mm or the kernel master page tables are modified to assign the addresses.

"map_vm_area()"
vmap_page_range
vmap_page_range_noflush
      This function takes out the page group descriptor for the address passed
      Subsequent callers map the page to the init_mm using various page table level calls

"vmap_p4d_range() -> vmap_p4d_range() -> vmap_pud_range() -> vmap_pmd_range() -> vmap_pte_range()".

Let's see how the resource map allocator finds the first suitable sized hole. The virtual address allocation can be seen in the "alloc_vmap_area()". The "vmap_area_root" is an rbtree (red black tree) sorted based on virtual address. The entries are taken from this rbtree to find the starting point of search. Once a starting point is found a sequential search is done for the suitable sized hole.

Let us write a program to see vmalloc use and ftrace it :

Kernel module:
```
#include<linux/mm.h>
#include<linux/vmalloc.h>

unsigned long addr;
int myinit(void)
{
```

```
        printk("module inserted\n");
        addr = vmalloc(2000);
        printk("VMALLOC_START = 0x%08lx, VMALLOC_END =
0x%08lx\n",
                VMALLOC_START, VMALLOC_END);
        printk("virtual address = 0x%08lx\n", addr);
        return 0;
}


void myexit(void)
{
        if(addr) {
                printk("free the memory\n");
                vfree(addr);
        }
        printk("module removed\n");
}


module_init(myinit);
module_exit(myexit);
```

Output :

```
Feb 27 17:41:51 x-vm kernel: [680963.914068] module
inserted
Feb 27 17:41:51 x-vm kernel: [680963.914092] VMALLOC_START
= 0xffffb47100000000, VMALLOC_END = 0xffffd470ffffffff
Feb 27 17:41:51 x-vm kernel: [680963.914095] virtual
address = 0xffffb471018cf000
Feb 27 17:41:54 x-vm kernel: [680966.086954] free the
memory
Feb 27 17:41:54 x-vm kernel: [680966.086967] module removed
```

Ftrace output:

```
7)                    |  vmalloc() {
7)                    |    __vmalloc_node_range() {
7)                    |      __get_vm_area_node() {
7)                    |        kmem_cache_alloc_node_trace() {
7)                    |          _cond_resched() {
```

```
7)   0.270 us    |              rcu_all_qs();
7)   1.300 us    |            }
7)   0.184 us    |            should_failslab();
7)   2.136 us    |          }
7)               |        alloc_vmap_area() {
7)               |          _cond_resched() {
7)   0.178 us    |            rcu_all_qs();
7)   0.518 us    |          }
7)               |          kmem_cache_alloc_node_trace()
{
7)               |            _cond_resched() {
7)   0.291 us    |              rcu_all_qs();
7)   0.630 us    |            }
7)   0.178 us    |            should_failslab();
7)   1.339 us    |          }
7)   0.220 us    |          _raw_spin_lock();
7)   0.478 us    |          __insert_vmap_area();
7)   4.512 us    |        }
7)   0.178 us    |        _raw_spin_lock();
7)   7.673 us    |      }
7)               |      __kmalloc_node() {
7)   0.178 us    |        kmalloc_slab();
7)               |        _cond_resched() {
7)   0.178 us    |          rcu_all_qs();
7)   0.629 us    |        }
7)   0.178 us    |        should_failslab();
7)   1.940 us    |      }
7)               |      alloc_pages_current() {
7)   0.178 us    |        get_task_policy.part.34();
7)   0.172 us    |        policy_nodemask();
7)   0.195 us    |        policy_node();
7)               |        __alloc_pages_nodemask() {
7)               |          _cond_resched() {
7)   0.178 us    |            rcu_all_qs();
7)   0.515 us    |          }
7)   0.175 us    |          should_fail_alloc_page();
7)               |          get_page_from_freelist() {
7)   0.200 us    |            __inc_numa_state();
```

```
7)    0.179 us    |                    __inc_numa_state();
7)    0.180 us    |                      kernel_poison_pages();
7)    0.178 us    |                      page_poisoning_enabled();
7)    2.227 us    |                  }
7)    3.779 us    |                }
7)    5.386 us    |              }
7)                |            _cond_resched() {
7)    0.178 us    |              rcu_all_qs();
7)    0.516 us    |            }
7)                |            map_vm_area() {
7)    0.332 us    |              vmap_page_range_noflush();
7)    0.795 us    |            }
7) + 17.711 us    |          }
7) + 19.285 us    |        }
```

Slab allocator

These allocations incur the least amount of internal fragmentation. The allocations done using this allocator are efficient and can be used for same sized object allocation.

We can create a unique slab for an object which gets allocated and deallocated frequently.

We can see that the Linux kernel creates slabs for many such objects.

Lets see them using "cat /proc/slabinfo" :

```
# name  <active_objs> <num_objs> <objsize> <objperslab>
<pagesperslab> : tunables <limit> <batchcount>
<sharedfactor> : slabdata <active_slabs> <num_slabs>
<sharedavail>
ext4_groupinfo_4k 560 560 144 28 1 : tunables 0 0 0 :
slabdata 20 20  0
PINGv6   0  0  1152  28 8 : tunables 0 0 0 : slabdata 0 0 0
RAWv6  112 112  1152  28 8 : tunables 0 0 0 : slabdata 4 4
0
UDPv6  200 200  1280  25 8 : tunables 0 0 0 : slabdata 8 8
0
```

```
tw_sock_TCPv6  0  0 240  34 2 : tunables 0 0 0 : slabdata 0
0 0
request_sock_TCPv6  0  0 304  26 2 : tunables 0 0 0 :
slabdata 0 0 0
TCPv6  104 104  2368  13 8 : tunables 0 0 0 : slabdata 8 8
0
kcopyd_job  0  0  3312 9 8 : tunables 0 0 0 : slabdata 0 0
0
dm_uevent   0  0  2632  12 8 : tunables 0 0 0 : slabdata 0
0 0
dm_old_clone_request  0  0 296  27 2 : tunables 0 0 0 :
slabdata 0 0 0
dm_rq_target_io  0  0 120  34 1 : tunables 0 0 0 : slabdata
0 0 0
scsi_sense_cache 1696 1696 128 32 1 : tunables 0 0 0 :
slabdata 53 53 0
mqueue_inode_cache  36  36 896  36 8 : tunables 0 0 0 :
slabdata 1 1 0
fuse_request  40  40 392  20 2 : tunables 0 0 0 : slabdata
2 2 0
fuse_inode  21  21 768  21 4 : tunables 0 0 0 : slabdata 1
1 0
…
…
```

vm_area_struct 2684 26840 200 20 1 : tunables 0 0 0 :
slabdata 1342 1342 0

mm_struct 240 240 1088 30 8 : tunables 0 0 0 : slabdata
8 8 0

files_cache 276 276 704 23 4 : tunables 0 0 0 : slabdata
12 12 0

signal_cache 780 780 1088 30 8 : tunables 0 0 0 :
slabdata 26 26 0

sighand_cache 495 495 2112 15 8 : tunables 0 0 0 :
slabdata 33 33 0

task_struct 611 650 5568 5 8 : tunables 0 0 0 : slabdata
130 130 0

…

…

```
kmalloc-8k    172 172   8192 4 8 : tunables 0 0 0 : slabdata
43 43 0
kmalloc-4k   1109  1152   4096 8 8 : tunables 0 0 0 :
slabdata 144 144 0
kmalloc-2k   2128 2128  2048 16 8 : tunables 0 0 0 :
slabdata 133 133 0
kmalloc-1k   1863  1984  1024 32 8 : tunables 0 0 0 :
slabdata  62 62 0
kmalloc-512  2816   2816 512  32 4 : tunables 0 0 0 :
slabdata  88 88 0
kmalloc-256   928 928 256  32 2 : tunables 0 0 0 : slabdata
29 29 0
kmalloc-192   2583  2583 192 21 1 : tunables 0 0 0 :
slabdata 123 123 0
kmalloc-128   1568  1568 128  32 1 : tunables 0 0 0 :
slabdata  49 49 0
kmalloc-96   4914   4914  96  42 1 : tunables 0 0 0 :
slabdata 117 117 0
kmalloc-64 12160 12160  64  64 1 : tunables 0 0 0 :
slabdata 190 190 0
kmalloc-32 14720 14720  32 128 1 : tunables 0 0 0 :
slabdata 115 115 0
kmalloc-16  9216  9216  16  256 1 : tunables 0 0 0 :
slabdata  36 36 0
kmalloc-8    8192  8192  8  512 1 : tunables 0 0 0 :
slabdata  16 16 0
kmem_cache_node  320 320  64  64 1 : tunables 0 0 0 :
slabdata 5 5 0
kmem_cache   189 189 384  21 2 : tunables 0 0 0 : slabdata
9 9 0
```

We can see that structures like "task_struct", "mm_struct" which get allocated and deallocated frequently are mentioned here. Also we see that we have pre-created slabs for kmalloc allocations

All these slabs or kmem_cache are created using "kmem_cache_create()" function. We can see its references in Linux kernel code :

```
0 pgtable.con.c    pgtable_cache_init                23
pgd_cachep =
kmem_cache_create("pgd_cache",
1 pgtable.c        pgtable_cache_init                27
pmd_cachep =
kmem_cache_create("pmd_cache",
```

Lets create a slab and allocate from it using these APIs

kmem_cache_create

kmem_cache_alloc

Kernel module to do the same :

```
#include<linux/module.h>
#include<linux/version.h>
#include<linux/kernel.h>
#include<linux/init.h>
#include<linux/gfp.h>
#include<linux/mm.h>
#include<linux/slab.h>


struct kmem_cache *my_cache = NULL;

struct my_struct {
    int a;
    int b;
    int c;
    int d;
};
struct my_struct *ptr = NULL;
int myinit(void)
{
```

```
        printk("module inserted\n");
        my_cache = kmem_cache_create("my_test_cache",
sizeof(struct my_struct), sizeof(struct my_struct), 0,
NULL);
        ptr = kmem_cache_zalloc(my_cache, GFP_KERNEL);
        printk("ptr address = 0x%08lx\n", ptr);
        return 0;
}

void myexit(void)
{
        if(ptr) {
                printk("free the object\n");
                kmem_cache_free(my_cache, ptr);
        }
        if(my_cache) {
                printk("free the cache\n");
                kmem_cache_destroy(my_cache);
        }
        printk("module removed\n");
}
module_init(myinit);
module_exit(myexit);
```

If we see the ftrace of "kmem_cache_alloc()" then we see that to finally allocate memory it also uses alloc_page/s.

Kmalloc

Many places we need to allocate in the form of smaller and varied size chunks of memory. For these types of allocations, the kernel creates default slabs of 8 bytes, 16 bytes, 32 bytes, 64 bytes etc. These default slabs are used for varied allocations. These slabs can be used using the kmalloc API.

If an allocation request of 8 or fewer bytes comes then it is fulfilled using a kmalloc slab of 8 bytes.

Allocation of 8 to 16 bytes is fulfilled using a kmalloc slab of 16 bytes. And so on it continues.

User space allocations

The user space programs use malloc API for allocations. These allocations do not allocate physical memory until touched. Once these are accessed/touched a page fault exception is raised by the MMU (memory management unit). Page fault exception results in instantaneous invocation of the page fault handler. Page fault starts demand paging for the requested address.

The function "do_page_fault()" is the page fault handler, and is called for any page fault. The memory address for which page fault occured is fetched from the CR2 register. CR2 register contains a value called Page Fault Linear Address (PFLA).When a page fault occurs, the address the program attempted to access is stored in the CR2 register.

Let's discuss the function graph of the page fault handler. "do_page_fault()" function calls "__do_page_fault()".
"__do_page_fault()" checks the validity of the address by checking if it exists after vma->vm_start. It also does many other checks and raises signal SEGV_MAPERR or SEGV_ACCERR.

If it is a good area (virtual address is correct) then it calls "handle_mm_fault()".
"__handle_mm_fault()" finds/allocates the PGD, PUD, PMD entries and calls the function "handle_pte_fault()", shown below :

```
static vm_fault_t handle_pte_fault(struct vm_fault *vmf)
{
...

. . .
if (!vmf->pte) {
                if (vma_is_anonymous(vmf->vma))
```

```
                    return do_anonymous_page(vmf);
            else
                    return do_fault(vmf);
     }

     if (!pte_present(vmf->orig_pte))
             return do_swap_page(vmf);

     if (pte_protnone(vmf->orig_pte) &&
vma_is_accessible(vmf->vma))
             return do_numa_page(vmf);
...
...
}
```

For the anonymous pages function "do_anonymous_page()" is getting called.

For writes it allocates a new page using "alloc_zeroed_user_highpage_movable()" :

```
/* Allocate our own private page. */
if (unlikely(anon_vma_prepare(vma)))
 goto oom;
page = alloc_zeroed_user_highpage_movable(vma, address);
if (!page)
 goto oom;
```

Eventually it will call "alloc_page()" and allocate a page from the buddy allocator.

```
static inline struct page *
alloc_zeroed_user_highpage_movable(struct vm_area_struct
*vma,
     unsigned long vaddr)
{
     return __alloc_zeroed_user_highpage(__GFP_MOVABLE, vma,
vaddr);
}
```

```
#define __alloc_zeroed_user_highpage(movableflags, vma,
vaddr) \
alloc_page_vma(GFP_HIGHUSER | __GFP_ZERO | movableflags,
vma, vaddr)


#define alloc_page_vma(gfp_mask, vma, addr)    \
alloc_pages_vma(gfp_mask, 0, vma, addr, numa_node_id(),
false)


#define alloc_pages_vma(gfp_mask, order, vma, addr, node,
false)\
alloc_pages(gfp_mask, order)
```

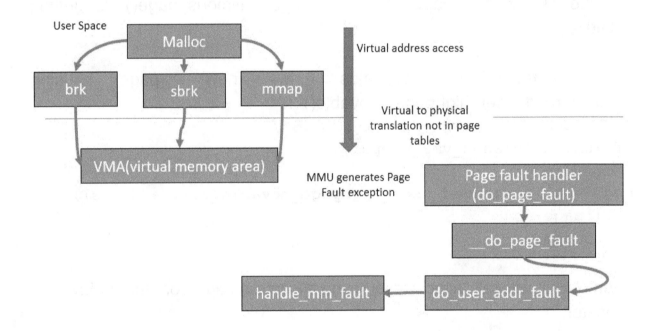

User space allocations triggering a page fault

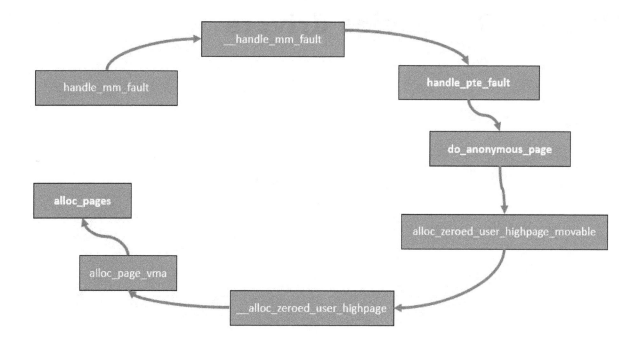

Page fault handler allocating actual pages

In principle we can see that :

1. All the allocators cater to different needs.
2. All of these allocations are based on the "alloc_page()" (the buddy allocator).

Chapter 9 Device drivers

Introduction

In this chapter we will go through the Linux framework using which device drivers are created. We will learn about Linux dynamic modules, Linux character driver framework, internal functions which are used while creating a character driver. We learn about UDEV events sent by a driver and also about its IOCTL interface.

We will also go through the Linux device model. Here we learn about bus, device and device_driver frameworks, which are the basis for Linux device model. We make a module which creates a sample bus, attaches a sample device to it and then loads a sample device driver for it. We will see a real time example of device model by going through the PCI bus framework of Linux.

Basic Linux module framework

In Linux, device drivers are made using Linux kernel module framework. In Linux we can write a loadable kernel module. We can insert and remove a module from the kernel at any point of time. Let's start with writing a Linux kernel module with just the init (initialization) and exit function. Unlike the Userspace program's "main()" function, this module has init and exit functions. As this is a kernel module, after insertion, the init and exit functions can access any internal global data structure of the kernel.

```c
#include <linux/kernel.h>
#include <linux/module.h>
#include <linux/types.h>
#include <linux/major.h>
#include <linux/kdev_t.h>
#include <linux/fs.h>

#include <linux/device.h>
#include <linux/cdev.h>
#include <linux/slab.h>

static int __init my_init(void)
{
```

```
    int ret = 0;

    printk("in init\n");
    return 0;
}

static void __exit my_exit(void)
{
    printk("in exit\n");
}


module_init(my_init);
module_exit(my_exit);
MODULE_AUTHOR("SampleAuthor");
MODULE_LICENSE("GPL");
```

Output :
```
Apr 23 22:49:48 x-server kernel: [5598016.247720] in init
Apr 23 22:50:22 x-server kernel: [5598050.557997] in exit
```

Basic character driver framework

In this section we will try to create a character device like "/dev/my_chr_drv".
Usage of a character driver :

1. These days it is mostly used to transfer control from user space to kernel space, When any user space application wants to access the data inside the kernel, or wants to know whether some data has arrived at the kernel then they use a character device.
2. A character device driver can be written with our own implementation of read, write, ioctl, open, close functions.

A character device is associated with a unique major and minor number, this serves as a unique key to index into the global hashmap of key value pairs. There is a global hashmap of all devices. The key of (maj, min) pair is used to index this global hashmap. The value in this hashmap is a data structure.

Lets create a full character driver and a corresponding device "/dev/my_chr_dev".

We generate first a MAJOR MINOR number for the character device file using the function "alloc_chrdev_region()".

```
ret = alloc_chrdev_region(&my_devt, 0, 1, drv_name);
if(ret == 0)
    printk("dev_t major is %d minor is %d\n",
MAJOR(my_devt), MINOR(my_devt));
```

Now we need to create a class using class create:

```
my_class = class_create(THIS_MODULE, "my_class");
if(my_class != NULL)
    printk("class created as %s\n", my_class->name);
```

This creates "/sys/class/my_class" to which the device shall be attached.

Now we will create a "struct device" and attach it to the class created :

```
my_chr_device = device_create(my_class, NULL, my_devt,
NULL, "my_chr_drv");
    if(my_chr_device != NULL)
        printk("device created dev_t as  %d\n",
my_chr_device->devt);
```

Next the device is associated with the file operations using "cdev_init()" function.

```
cdev_init(&my_cdev, &myfops);
```

And the character device data structure is associated with the major and minor numbers we allocated in the beginning of this program.

```
cdev_add(&my_cdev, my_devt, 1);
```

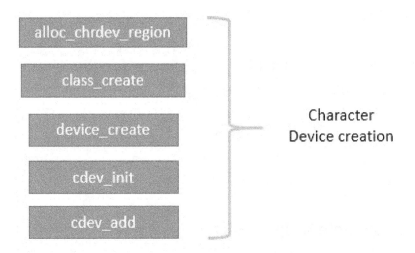

Steps in creation of a character device

Internals of device_create() function

The "device_create()" function is an important function which creates "sys" entries for a device and the "/dev/my_chr_dev entry". Let's see its internal function calls.

```
device_create(my_class, NULL, my_devt, NULL, "my_chr_drv");
    device_create_vargs
    device_create_groups_vargs
            struct device is allocated.
            device_add is called for the struct device
    created.
        device_add
            device_create_file
                sysfs_create_file
            device_add_class_symlinks
            bus_add_device
            devtmpfs_create_node
            kobject_uevent(&dev->kobj, KOBJ_ADD)
            bus_probe_device
```

"devtmpfs_create_node" function is responsible for creation of device node:
The creation of "/dev/" entry is done by a kernel thread "kdevtmpfs".

Associating the device with the file operations

There are two functions which help to associate a character device with its file operations.

```
cdev_init(&my_cdev, &myfops);
cdev_add(&my_cdev, my_devt, 1);
```

"cdev_init" assigns the "file_operations" to the cdev data structure :
```
cdev->ops = fops;
```

How do the read and write file operations get called for this character device?

The following diagram illustrates the same:

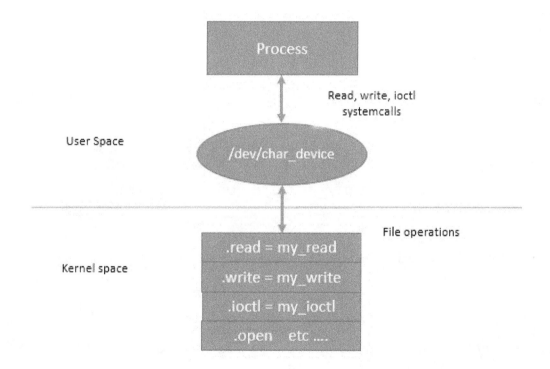

Complete illustration

```c
#include <linux/kernel.h>
#include <linux/module.h>
#include <linux/types.h>
#include <linux/major.h>
#include <linux/kdev_t.h>
#include <linux/fs.h>

#include <linux/device.h>
#include <linux/cdev.h>
#include <linux/slab.h>
#include <linux/uaccess.h>

char global_buf[20];

dev_t my_devt;
char drv_name[] = "my_chr_drv";
struct class *my_class;
struct cdev my_cdev;
struct device *my_chr_device;

ssize_t my_read (struct file *myfile, char __user *my_buf,
size_t len, loff_t *off)
{
    int ret;
    ret = copy_to_user(my_buf, global_buf, len);
    if(ret != 0)
        printk("not able to copy\n");
    printk("copied the data to user buffer\n");
    return len;
}

ssize_t my_write (struct file *my_file, const char __user
*buf, size_t len, loff_t *off)
{

    int ret;
```

```
    ret = copy_from_user(global_buf, buf, len);
    if(ret != 0)
        printk("not able to copy\n");
    printk("copied the data from user buffer\n");
    return len;
}

struct file_operations myfops = {
    .owner = THIS_MODULE,
    .read = my_read,
    .write = my_write,
};

static int __init my_init(void)
{
    int ret = 0;
    printk("in init\n");

    ret = alloc_chrdev_region(&my_devt, 0, 1, drv_name);
    if(ret == 0)
     printk("dev_t major is %d minor is %d\n",
MAJOR(my_devt), MINOR(my_devt));

    my_class =  class_create(THIS_MODULE, "my_class");
    if(my_class != NULL)
     printk("class created as %s\n", my_class->name);

    my_chr_device = device_create(my_class, NULL, my_devt,
NULL, "my_chr_drv");
    if(my_chr_device != NULL)
     printk("device created dev_t as  %d\n", my_chr_device->devt);

    cdev_init(&my_cdev, &myfops);
    cdev_add(&my_cdev, my_devt, 1);
    return 0;
}
```

```
static void __exit my_exit(void)
{
    printk("in exit\n");
    cdev_del(&my_cdev);
    if(my_chr_device != NULL)
        device_destroy(my_class, my_devt);
    if(my_class != NULL)
        class_destroy(my_class);
    if(my_devt != 0)
        unregister_chrdev_region(my_devt,1);
}


module_init(my_init);
module_exit(my_exit);
MODULE_AUTHOR("SampleAuthor");
MODULE_LICENSE("GPL");
```

Commands used to load, read, write and unload the module:

```
root@x-server:~/driver/s2# insmod simple.ko
root@x-server:~/driver/s1# lsmod | grep simple
simple                 16384   0

 dd if=/dev/zero bs=5 count=1 of=/dev/my_chr_drv <== Write
to the device
 dd if=/dev/my_chr_drv  bs=5 count=1 of=/dev/null <== Read
from the device
root@x-server:~/driver/s1# rmmod simple
```

Output

```
Apr 23 23:14:02 x-server kernel: [5599470.134684] in init
Apr 23 23:14:02 x-server kernel: [5599470.134691] dev_t
major is 237 minor is 0
Apr 23 23:14:02 x-server kernel: [5599470.134718] class
created as my_class

Apr 23 23:14:02 x-server kernel: [5599470.134995] device
created dev_t as  248512512
```

```
Apr 23 23:29:40 x-server kernel: [5600407.898987] copied
the data from user buffer
Apr 23 23:35:46 x-server kernel: [5600773.710579] copied
the data to user buffer
Apr 23 23:38:37 x-server kernel: [5600945.230631] in exit
```

UDEV

We saw the creation of the character driver making a call to "kobject_uevent" is made.

```
kobject_uevent(&dev->kobj, KOBJ_ADD);
```

This call sends a netlink message from kernel space to user space over netlink socket. This message transmission is referred to as a UDEV event.

At User space, this message is received by UDEV daemon, Udevd (a daemon now a part of systemd). For the message received at User space, UDEV rules are executed per device. Lets see in detail the running of UDEV rules.

Udev rules :

These are files present in "/lib/udev/rules.d/". There are several "*.rules" files present in this directory. Let's take a look at the files present in this directory.

```
root@x-server:/lib/udev/rules.d# ls
39-usbmuxd.rules                 66-snapd-
autoimport.rules                 77-mm-usb-serial-adapters-
greylist.rules
40-usb-media-players.rules       69-cd-sensors.rules
77-mm-x22x-port-types.rules
```

Each rule file can have multiple statements. Each line of the UDEV rule is of the format CHECK, ACTION

Example 1:

```
KERNEL=="device-mapper", NAME="mapper/control"
```

This rule says that if the device name "/dev/device-mapper" is getting created then a device naemd " /dev/mapper/control" also needs to be created.

Example 2:

```
ENV{DM_COOKIE}=="?*",        IMPORT{program}="/usr/sbin/dmsetup
udevflags $env{DM_COOKIE}"
```

This rule says if ENV variable DM_COOKIE is present then execute a command

Capturing UDEV events

We can capture/sniff all the udev events getting generated in the kernel using the "udevadm" utility.

```
# udevadm monitor -p
```

This utility listens on the netlink socket and prints the events coming from the kernel.

Miscellaneous character driver

A simple character driver can be created using the misc_register and misc_deregister calls.
In this section we will form a sample miscellaneous character device. Using this miscellaneous character device we will try to call its ioctl function. Let's see this ioctl example.

IOCTL

Ioctl is a way to pass any custom command from user space to the kernel. Passing an ioctl command will require making a custom ioctl function available in file_operations of the character device.

Framework for IOCTL

When the user space program calls "ioctl()" on the character device, the custom device function "my_ioctl()" is called. The "my_ioctl()" function is assigned to the "file_operation" of the character device driver.

```
struct file_operations myfops = {
...

...

    .unlocked_ioctl = my_ioctl
};
```

The command number for IOCTL is generated using macros _IOR, _IOW etc. These macros help to generate a unique command number that is to be passed from user space to the kernel.

Example of IOCTL command number generation:
```
#define FIRST_IOCTL _IOR(MY_MAGIC, 0, int)
#define SECOND_IOCTL _IOR(MY_MAGIC, 1, int)
```

Definition of ioctl function

The ioctl command numbers are passed to the kernel ioctl function as "unsigned int cmd".
```
long my_ioctl(struct file *file, unsigned int cmd, unsigned
long arg)
{
    switch(cmd) {
            case FIRST_IOCTL:
                    printk("first ioctl\n");
                    break;
            case SECOND_IOCTL:
                    printk("second ioctl\n");
                    break;
            default:
                    return -ENOTTY;
    }
    return 0;
};
```

The complete sample driver program :

```c
#include <linux/module.h>
#include <linux/init.h>
#include <linux/kernel.h>
#include <linux/fs.h>
#include <linux/uaccess.h>
#include <linux/device.h>
#include <linux/miscdevice.h>

#define MY_MAGIC 'K'
#define FIRST_IOCTL _IOR(MY_MAGIC, 0, int)
#define SECOND_IOCTL _IOR(MY_MAGIC, 1, int)

long trial_ioctl(struct file *file, unsigned int cmd,
unsigned long arg)
{
        switch(cmd) {
                case FIRST_IOCTL:
                        printk("first ioctl\n");
                        break;
                case SECOND_IOCTL:
                        printk("second ioctl\n");
                        break;
                default:
                        return -ENOTTY;
        }
        return 0;
}

static const struct file_operations trial_fops={
        .owner = THIS_MODULE,
        .unlocked_ioctl = trial_ioctl
};

static struct miscdevice misc_struct={
        .minor = MISC_DYNAMIC_MINOR,
        .name = "trial_device",
        .fops = &trial_fops,
```

```
};

static int __init func_init(void)
{
        int result = 0;
        result = misc_register(&misc_struct);
        if (result<0)
                printk("misc_register error ");
        else
                printk("device registered with minor number
= %i \n" , misc_struct.minor);
        return result ;
}

static void __exit func_exit(void)
{
        misc_deregister(&misc_struct) ;
        printk("device unregistered");
}

module_init(func_init);
module_exit(func_exit);

MODULE_AUTHOR("SampleAuthor");
MODULE_DESCRIPTION("misc character driver");
```

Let's call it from a user space program:

```
#include <stdio.h>
#include <stdlib.h>
#include <string.h>
#include <sys/types.h>
#include <sys/stat.h>
#include <sys/ioctl.h>
#include <unistd.h>
#include <fcntl.h>
#include <errno.h>
```

```
#define MY_MAGIC 'K'
#define FIRST_IOCTL _IOR(MY_MAGIC, 0, int)
#define SECOND_IOCTL _IOR(MY_MAGIC, 1, int)

int main()
{
        int fd = -1, ret;

        fd = open("/dev/trial_device", O_RDWR);
        ret = ioctl(fd, FIRST_IOCTL, NULL);
        ret = ioctl(fd, SECOND_IOCTL, NULL);

        return 0;
}
```

Output at the kernel :
```
Apr 28 00:00:46 x-server kernel: [5947874.513257] first
ioctl
Apr 28 00:00:46 x-server kernel: [5947874.513269] second
ioctl
```

Linux Device model

Linux device model defines generic interfaces for device, bus and device_driver.

Generic device interface

The generic device is represented using the following structure.
```
struct device {
    ...
    struct kobject kobj;
    ...
    struct bus_type * bus;
```

```
    ...
    struct device_driver *driver;
};
```

We saw the creation of a "struct device" at the time of "device_create" call, while creating a character device.

Generic bus interface

A generic bus interface is represented using the following structure:

```
struct bus_type {
    const char * name;
    ...
    int (*match)(struct device * dev, struct device_driver
* drv);
    int (*uevent)(struct device *dev, struct
kobj_uevent_env *env);
    int (*probe)(struct device * dev);
    ...
    ...
};
```

Generic device_driver interface

A generic device_driver interface is represented using the following structure:

```
struct device_driver {
    const char              *name;
    struct bus_type          *bus;
...
}
```

BUS creation

In Linux, bus creation is done using the bus_register function. After the creation of a bus, devices can be attached to the bus using device_add() function.

First, we need to create a bus device and bus_type data structures.

```
struct device my_bus =
{
    .init_name = "my_bus",
    .release = my_bus_release
};


struct bus_type my_bus_type =
{
    .name = "my_bus",
    .match = my_bus_match
    .uevent = my_bus_uevent,
};
```

Then we can register the bus using the bus_register function.

```
device_register(&my_bus)
ret = bus_register(&my_bus_type);
```

All bus creations in the Linux kernel are done using "bus_register()". Lets see the references of "bus_register()" in the Linux kernel.

2 bus.c   **acpi_bus_init**   1215 result =
bus_register(&acpi_bus_type);
3 bus.c   amba_init   212 return
bus_register(&amba_bustype);
4 bus.c   bus_register   851 int bus_register(struct
bus_type *bus)
5 bus.c   subsys_register   1153 err =
bus_register(subsys);

6 isa.c **isa_bus_init** 175 error = bus_register(&isa_bus_type);

7 platform.c platform_bus_init 1176 error = bus_register(&platform_bus_type);

8 domain.c genpd_bus_init 2650 return bus_register(&genpd_bus_type);

9 soc.c soc_bus_register 174 ret = bus_register(&soc_bus_type);

a main.c bcma_init_bus_register 679 err = bus_register(&bcma_bus_type);

b rbd.c rbd_sysfs_init 6081 ret = bus_register(&rbd_bus_type);

c fsl-mc-bus.c fsl_mc_bus_driver_init 927 error = bus_register(&fsl_mc_bus_type);

d mips_cdmm.c mips_cdmm_init 672 ret = bus_register(&mips_cdmm_bustype);

Next devices are attached to a bus, using "device_add()".

Attach device to bus

We need to allocate a "struct device" and fill the bus details into it. Then we call "device_add()". Doing this attaches the device to the bus's list of devices.

```
my_device = kzalloc(sizeof(struct device), GFP_KERNEL);
device_initialize(my_device);
my_device->parent = &my_bus;
my_device->bus = &my_bus_type;
my_device->init_name = "my_chr_dev";
ret = device_add(my_device);
```

Device_driver structure and its registration

The "device_driver" structure shall be assigned a bustype and the probe function. Then it can be registered using the driver_register function.

```
struct device_driver my_dev_driver = {
    .owner = THIS_MODULE,
    .name = "my_chr_drv",
    .bus = &my_bus_type
    .probe = my_driver_probe,
    .probe_type = PROBE_FORCE_SYNCHRONOUS,
    .remove = my_driver_remove,
};
```

driver_register(&my_dev_driver);

The registration of "device_driver" performs a sequence of events. We will see these in the following sample program.

Device Model Example

In the following program we will create a sample bus, attach a sample device to it and register a sample driver for it.

```
#include <linux/kernel.h>
#include <linux/module.h>
#include <linux/types.h>
#include <linux/major.h>
#include <linux/kdev_t.h>
#include <linux/fs.h>

#include <linux/device.h>
#include <linux/cdev.h>
#include <linux/slab.h>
#include <linux/semaphore.h>
#include <linux/uaccess.h>

dev_t my_devt;

char drv_name[] = "my_chr_drv";
struct class *my_class;
```

```
struct device *my_device;
struct device *my_chr_device;

char global_buf[20];

struct my_super_device
{
    struct cdev my_cdev;
    int count;
    struct semaphore my_sem;
};


struct my_super_device *my_super;

ssize_t my_read (struct file *myfile, char __user *my_buf,
size_t len, loff_t *off)
{
    int ret;
    //printk("len = %d\n",len);
    ret = copy_to_user(my_buf, global_buf, len);
    if(ret != 0)
        printk("not able to copy\n");
    printk("copied the data to user buffer\n");
    return len;
}

ssize_t my_write (struct file *my_file, const char __user
*buf, size_t len, loff_t *off)
{
    int ret;
    ret = copy_from_user(global_buf, buf, len);
    if(ret != 0)
        printk("not able to copy\n");
    printk("copied the data from user buffer\n");
    return len;
}
```

```c
int my_mmap (struct file *my_file, struct vm_area_struct
*my_vm)
{
    return 0;
}


int my_open (struct inode *my_inode, struct file *my_file)
{
    struct my_super_device *super_ptr;
    printk("open called\n");
    printk("cdev address = %p\n", my_inode->i_cdev);

    super_ptr = container_of(my_inode->i_cdev, struct
my_super_device, my_cdev);
    up(&(super_ptr->my_sem));
    printk("super address = %p\n", super_ptr);
    return 0;
}


int my_release (struct inode *my_inode, struct file
*my_file)
{
    struct my_super_device *super_ptr;
    printk("release called\n");

    super_ptr = container_of(my_inode->i_cdev, struct
my_super_device, my_cdev);
    down(&(super_ptr->my_sem));
    return 0;
}


unsigned int my_poll (struct file *my_file, struct
poll_table_struct *poll_table)
{
    return 0;
}


struct file_operations myfops = {
```

```c
    .owner = THIS_MODULE,
    .read = my_read,
    .write = my_write,
    .poll = my_poll,
    .open = my_open,
    .release = my_release,
};

int my_bus_match(struct device *dev, struct device_driver
*drv)
{
    printk("Entered %s\n",__func__);
    return 1;
}
int my_bus_uevent(struct device *dev, struct
kobj_uevent_env *env)
{
    printk("Entered %s\n",__func__);
    return 0;
}

void my_bus_release(struct device *dev)
{
    printk("Entered %s\n",__func__);
    return ;
}

struct device my_bus = {
        .init_name = "my_bus",
    .release = my_bus_release,
};

struct bus_type my_bus_type = {
    .name = "my_bus",
    .match = my_bus_match,
    .uevent = my_bus_uevent,
};
```

```
int my_driver_probe(struct device *dev)
{
    int ret;

    printk("Entered %s\n",__func__);

    ret = alloc_chrdev_region(&my_devt, 0, 1, drv_name);
    if(ret == 0)
            printk("dev_t major is %d minor is %d\n",
MAJOR(my_devt), MINOR(my_devt));
    dev->devt = my_devt;
    my_class =  class_create(THIS_MODULE, "my_class");
    if(my_class != NULL)
            printk("class created as %s\n", my_class-
>name);

    my_chr_device = device_create(my_class, NULL, my_devt,
NULL, "my_chr_drv");
    if(my_chr_device != NULL)
            printk("device created dev_t as  %d\n",
my_chr_device->devt);

    my_super = kzalloc(sizeof(struct my_super_device),
GFP_KERNEL);
    sema_init(&(my_super->my_sem), 1);
    cdev_init(&(my_super->my_cdev), &myfops);
    cdev_add(&(my_super->my_cdev), my_devt, 1);
    return 0;
}

int my_driver_remove(struct device *dev)
{
    printk("Entered %s\n",__func__);

    if(my_chr_device != NULL)
        device_destroy(my_class, my_devt);
    if(my_class != NULL)
        class_destroy(my_class);
```

```c
    if(my_devt != 0)
        unregister_chrdev_region(my_devt,1);

    return 0;
}

struct device_driver my_dev_driver = {
    .owner = THIS_MODULE,
    .name = "my_chr_drv",
    .bus = &my_bus_type,
    .probe = my_driver_probe,
    .probe_type = PROBE_FORCE_SYNCHRONOUS,
    .remove = my_driver_remove,
};

static int __init my_init(void)
{
    int ret = 0;

    printk("in init\n");

    /*Register the bus*/
    ret = device_register(&my_bus);
    if(ret == 0)
        printk("device registered correctly\n");
    else
        printk("ret = %d\n",ret);

    ret = bus_register(&my_bus_type);
    if(ret == 0)
        printk("bus registered correctly\n");
    else
        printk("ret = %d\n",ret);

    /*add device for the device driver*/
    my_device = kzalloc(sizeof(struct device), GFP_KERNEL);
    device_initialize(my_device);
```

```
    my_device->parent = &my_bus;
    my_device->bus = &my_bus_type;
    my_device->init_name = "my_chr_dev";

    ret = device_add(my_device);
    if(ret == 0)
        printk("device added correctly\n");
    else
        printk("ret = %d\n",ret);

    /*Now register the driver*/
    ret = driver_register(&my_dev_driver);
    if(ret == 0)
        printk("driver registered correctly\n");
    else
        printk("ret = %d\n",ret);

    return 0;
}

static void __exit my_exit(void)
{
    printk("in exit\n");
    driver_unregister(&my_dev_driver);
    bus_unregister(&my_bus_type);
    device_unregister(&my_bus);
}

module_init(my_init);
module_exit(my_exit);
MODULE_AUTHOR("SampleAuthor");
MODULE_LICENSE("GPL");
```

Output of this program :

```
Apr 28 01:37:14 x-server kernel: [5953662.343927] in init
Apr 28 01:37:14 x-server kernel: [5953662.343982] device registered correctly
Apr 28 01:37:14 x-server kernel: [5953662.344022] bus registered correctly
Apr 28 01:37:14 x-server kernel: [5953662.344089] Entered my_bus_uevent
Apr 28 01:37:14 x-server kernel: [5953662.344106] device added correctly
```

```
Apr 28 01:37:14 x-server kernel: [5953662.344116] Entered my_bus_match
Apr 28 01:37:14 x-server kernel: [5953662.344137] Entered my_driver_probe
Apr 28 01:37:14 x-server kernel: [5953662.344142] dev_t major is 237 minor is
0
Apr 28 01:37:14 x-server kernel: [5953662.344163] class created as my_class
Apr 28 01:37:14 x-server kernel: [5953662.344379] device created dev_t as
248512512
Apr 28 01:37:14 x-server kernel: [5953662.344409] Entered my_bus_uevent
Apr 28 01:37:14 x-server kernel: [5953662.344455] driver registered correctly
Apr 28 01:37:14 x-server kernel: [5953662.352360] Entered my_bus_uevent
Apr 28 01:37:14 x-server kernel: [5953662.356423] Entered my_bus_uevent

Apr 28 01:38:36 x-server kernel: [5953743.626629] in exit
Apr 28 01:38:36 x-server kernel: [5953743.626681] Entered my_driver_remove
Apr 28 01:38:36 x-server kernel: [5953743.627067] Entered my_bus_uevent
```

Tracing the driver_register call tells us the sequence of function calls which takes place for this program.

```
# tracer: function_graph
#
# CPU   DURATION                  FUNCTION CALLS
# |      |    |                      |   |   |   |
 18)                    |  driver_register() {
 18)                    |    driver_find() {
 18)   0.246 us         |      _raw_spin_lock();
 18)   1.076 us         |    }
 18)                    |    bus_add_driver() {

...
...
...
...
 18)                    |            driver_attach() {
 18)                    |              bus_for_each_dev() {
 18)   0.166 us         |                _raw_spin_lock_irqsave();
 18)   0.175 us         |
_raw_spin_unlock_irqrestore();
 18)                    |                __driver_attach() {
 18)                    |                  my_bus_match [bus]() {
```

```
18)                   |                  printk() {
18)                   |                    vprintk_func() {
18)                   |                      vprintk_default() {
18)   1.807 us        |                        vprintk_emit();
18)   2.135 us        |                      }
18)   2.904 us        |                    }
18)   3.264 us        |                  }
18)   3.680 us        |                }
18)                   |                mutex_lock() {
18)                   |                  _cond_resched() {
18)   0.179 us        |                    rcu_all_qs();
18)   0.629 us        |                  }
18)   0.984 us        |                }
18)                   |                driver_probe_device() {
18)                   |
pm_runtime_get_suppliers() {
18)                   |
device_links_read_lock() {
18)   0.335 us        |                      __srcu_read_lock();
18)   0.716 us        |                    }
18)                   |
device_links_read_unlock() {
18)   0.243 us        |                      __srcu_read_unlock();
18)   0.585 us        |                    }
18)   1.941 us        |                  }
18)                   |                  __pm_runtime_resume() {
18)                   |                    _cond_resched() {
18)   0.157 us        |                      rcu_all_qs();
18)   0.483 us        |                    }
18)   0.161 us        |
_raw_spin_lock_irqsave();
18)   0.179 us        |                    rpm_resume();
18)   0.181 us        |
_raw_spin_unlock_irqrestore();
18)   1.842 us        |                  }
18)                   |                  pm_runtime_barrier() {
18)   0.162 us        |                    _raw_spin_lock_irq();
18)   0.177 us        |                    __pm_runtime_barrier();
```

```
18)    0.869 us   |                          }
...
...
18)               |              my_driver_probe [bus]()
{
18)               |                  printk() {
18)    1.743 us   |                    vprintk_func();
18)    2.052 us   |                  }
18)               |                  alloc_chrdev_region()
{
18)    0.802 us   |
__register_chrdev_region();
18)    1.241 us   |                  }
18)               |                  printk() {
18)    1.990 us   |                    vprintk_func();
18)    2.297 us   |                  }
18)               |                  __class_create() {
18)    0.367 us   |
kmem_cache_alloc_trace();
18) + 12.172 us   |                    __class_register();
18) + 13.015 us   |                  }
18)               |                  printk() {
18)    1.660 us   |                    vprintk_func();
18)    1.974 us   |                  }
18)               |                  device_create() {
18) ! 155.752 us  |
device_create_groups_vargs();
18) ! 156.246 us  |                  }
18)               |                  printk() {
18)    2.122 us   |                    vprintk_func();
18)    2.982 us   |                  }
18)               |
kmem_cache_alloc_trace() {
18)    0.306 us   |                    _cond_resched();
18)    0.169 us   |                    should_failslab();
18)    0.996 us   |                  }
18)    0.193 us   |                  cdev_init();
18)               |                  cdev_add() {
```

```
18)    0.971 us   |                      kobj_map();
18)    1.438 us   |                    }
18)  ! 184.928 us |                  }
..
...
...
18)    0.181 us   |
blocking_notifier_call_chain();
18)    0.178 us   |                      dev_uevent_filter();
18)    0.179 us   |                      dev_uevent_name();
18)               |
kmem_cache_alloc_trace() {
18)    9.097 us   |                        _cond_resched();
18)    0.177 us   |                        should_failslab();
18)    9.878 us   |                      }
...
...

18)               |                  module_add_driver() {
18)               |                    sysfs_create_link() {
18)               |
sysfs_do_create_link_sd.isra.2() {
18)    0.151 us   |                        _raw_spin_lock();
18)    0.164 us   |                        kernfs_get();
18)               |                        kernfs_create_link() {
18)               |                          kernfs_new_node() {
18)               |                            __kernfs_new_node() {
18)    0.170 us   |                              kstrdup_const();
18)               |                              kmem_cache_alloc() {
...
...
18)               |                    driver_create_file() {
18)               |                      sysfs_create_file_ns() {
18)               |                        sysfs_add_file_mode_ns() {
18)               |                          __kernfs_create_file() {
18)               |                            kernfs_new_node() {
18)               |                              __kernfs_new_node() {
18)    0.148 us   |                                kstrdup_const();
```

```
18)                          |                      kmem_cache_alloc() {
18)      0.200 us            |                        _cond_resched();
18)      0.154 us            |                        should_failslab();
18)      0.832 us            |                      }
18)      0.153 us            |                      _raw_spin_lock();
18)      1.869 us            |                    }
18)      0.154 us            |                  kernfs_get();
18)      2.495 us            |                }
18)                          |              kernfs_add_one() {
18)                          |                mutex_lock() {
18)                          |                  _cond_resched() {
18)      0.156 us            |                    rcu_all_qs();
18)      0.448 us            |                  }
18)      0.749 us            |                }
18)      0.183 us            |                kernfs_name_hash();
18)      0.205 us            |                kernfs_link_sibling();
18)      0.153 us            |                mutex_unlock();
18)                          |                kernfs_activate() {
18)                          |                  mutex_lock() {
18)      0.197 us            |                    _cond_resched();
18)      0.498 us            |                  }
18)      0.162 us            |
kernfs_next_descendant_post();
18)      0.163 us            |
kernfs_next_descendant_post();
18)      0.154 us            |                  mutex_unlock();
18)      1.742 us            |                }
18)      3.947 us            |              }
18)      6.906 us            |            }
18)      7.226 us            |          }
18)      7.549 us            |        }
18)      7.843 us            |      }
18)                          |      driver_add_groups() {
18)      0.158 us            |        sysfs_create_groups();
18)      0.470 us            |      }
18)                          |      driver_create_file() {
..
...
```

. . .

Sequence of functions after driver_register()

PCI Bus enumeration

In the previous section we dealt with the creation of bus, devices and "device_driver". Lets see these things in reality. In this section we will see an example of PCI bus registration; how the "device_driver" is loaded for the devices present on the PCI bus.

Lets depict a very simple representation of PCI bus.

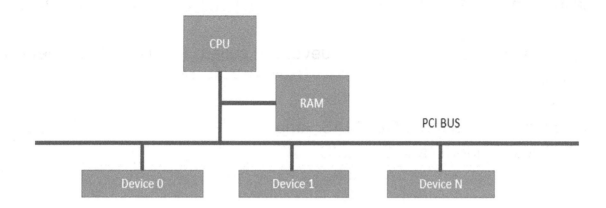

For this kind of bus architecture, the operating system shall perform the following steps:

1.　Find how many devices are attached on the PCI bus
2.　For each device load the needed driver
3.　Each driver starts the functioning of the device.

Finding Devices on PCI bus

On a PCI bus one can read the VendorID and DeviceID of a device. If the VendorID and DeviceID are not 0xFFFFFFFF then we can tell that an actual device is attached to a PCI Slot.

Each PCI device has a PCI bus number, device number and function number. In a system we can have a maximum of 256 PCI buses, each bus having a maximum of 32 devices and each device having 8 functions.

The operating system tries to read the VendorID and DeviceID for each valid combination of bus, device and function. Using this brute force approach, if it finds a valid VendorId and DeviceID then it says the device is present on the PCI device.

In the Linux kernel this enumeration of devices is done using the "pci_scan_slot()" function. For each device the "pci_device_add()" function is called, which in turn calls device_add() function to attach the device to the bus.

Also for each attached device "pci_uevent" is called. This is the bus's uevent function.

This function sends the MODALIAS variable. The MODALIAS variable has the device's VendorID and DeviceID.

```
static int pci_uevent(struct device *dev, struct
kobj_uevent_env *env)
{
        struct pci_dev *pdev;
..

...

        if (add_uevent_var(env,
"MODALIAS=pci:v%08Xd%08Xsv%08Xsd%08Xbc%02Xsc%02Xi%02X",
                        pdev->vendor, pdev->device,
                        pdev->subsystem_vendor, pdev-
>subsystem_device,
                        (u8)(pdev->class >> 16),
(u8)(pdev->class >> 8),
                        (u8)(pdev->class)))
                return -ENOMEM;

        return 0;
}
```

This uevent is captured by UDEVD. Udevd looks inside "/lib/modules/<kernel>/modules.alias" for the driver present for this PCI device. The contents of modules.alias file is in the format VendorIDDeviceID <driver name>. Then Udevd loads the driver.

Illustration of the contents of modules.alias:

```
..
alias pci:v00008086d000010C4sv*sd*bc*sc*i* e1000e
alias pci:v00008086d000010C5sv*sd*bc*sc*i* e1000e
alias pci:v00008086d0000104Csv*sd*bc*sc*i* e1000e
alias pci:v00008086d000010BBsv*sd*bc*sc*i* e1000e
```

..

As the driver is loaded, it starts performing device specific initialization. This gets the PCI device working.

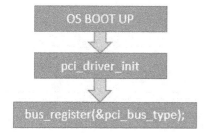
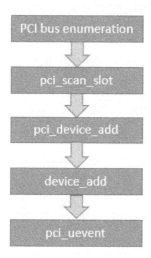
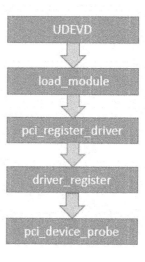

Chapter 10 Linux Block IO

In this chapter we will see all the layers through which an IO traverse.
We will write a simple C program and write to file. We will see how the write is given to the disk,
what are the layers through which the IO traverses.

To start this exercise we will be using one of the device files from the "/dev/" folder. These are special files which represent nodes of the filesystem tree. If one goes through the output of the command "ls -l /dev/", one can find a number of these device files. Not all of them are similar, some are block devices, some are character devices, or soft links. Every device file has two numbers associated with it. A major and a minor number.
In simple terms the major number is used to identify the driver (and the protocol possibly?) associated with that device file. From the kernel's perspective, the major number is the offset that can be used to retrieve the gendisk structure (include/linux/genhd.h) for that device. The gendisk structure is used to store a disk device's kernel representation. For a block device this is done by using the "get_gendisk()" function, which in turn uses the "kobj_lookup()" function.

```
struct gendisk *get_gendisk(dev_t devt, int *partno)
{
    struct gendisk *disk = NULL;

    if (MAJOR(devt) != BLOCK_EXT_MAJOR) {
        struct kobject *kobj;

        kobj = kobj_lookup(bdev_map, devt, partno);
        if (kobj)
            disk = dev_to_disk(kobj_to_dev(kobj));
.
```

The minor number is used to uniquely identify a particular device file among all the device files of the same type (having the same major number).

For this exercise we will be taking a block device file.

```
# ls -l /dev/sd*
brw-rw---- 1 root disk 8,  0 Feb 13 08:13 /dev/sda
brw-rw---- 1 root disk 8,  1 Feb 13 08:13 /dev/sda1
brw-rw---- 1 root disk 8, 16 Feb 13 08:13 /dev/sdb
brw-rw---- 1 root disk 8, 32 Feb 13 08:13 /dev/sdc
```

A sample program

Let us make a file system on the entire disk "sdc". For this example we are using ext4 filesystem.

```
# mkfs.ext4 /dev/sdc
mke2fs 1.44.6 (5-Mar-2019)
Creating filesystem with 2621440 4k blocks and 655360
inodes
Filesystem UUID: fb03438b-6174-4a78-89df-3d5baf5d7d19
Superblock backups stored on blocks:
        32768, 98304, 163840, 229376, 294912, 819200,
884736, 1605632

Allocating group tables: done
Writing inode tables: done
Creating journal (16384 blocks): done
Writing superblocks and filesystem accounting information:
done
```

Let us mount the filesystem on a directory and try to write to a file in that directory.

```
# mount /dev/sdc /mnt
```

In our C program we will write to a file in the "/mnt" directory using O_SYNC. When the O_SYNC flag is used the file is opened for synchronous I/O. Any write's on the resulting file descriptor will block the calling process until the data has been physically written to the underlying hardware.

```
#include <sys/types.h>
```

```c
#include <sys/stat.h>
#include <fcntl.h>
#include <unistd.h>

int main(void)
{
        int fd, ret;
        char buf[20] =
{'X','X','X','X','X','X','X','X','X','X','X','X','X','X','X
','X','X','X','X','X'};

        fd = open("/mnt/a",
O_RDWR|O_SYNC|O_APPEND|O_CREAT);
        write(fd, buf, 20);
        close(fd);
        return 0;
}
```

Running the above program with strace, which will enable us to see the system calls made by that program to complete the "write".

```
# strace ./a.out
execve("./a.out", ["./a.out"], 0x7fff256bb100 /* 19 vars
*/) = 0
brk(NULL)                               = 0x56225feee000
access("/etc/ld.so.preload", R_OK)      = -1 ENOENT (No
such file or directory)
openat(AT_FDCWD, "/etc/ld.so.cache", O_RDONLY|O_CLOEXEC) =
3
fstat(3, {st_mode=S_IFREG|0644, st_size=89340, ...}) = 0
mmap(NULL, 89340, PROT_READ, MAP_PRIVATE, 3, 0) =
0x7fabec870000
close(3)                                = 0
openat(AT_FDCWD, "/lib/x86_64-linux-gnu/libc.so.6",
O_RDONLY|O_CLOEXEC) = 3
read(3,
"\177ELF\2\1\1\3\0\0\0\0\0\0\0\0\3\0>\0\1\0\0\0\2001\2\0\0\
0\0\0"..., 832) = 832
```

```
fstat(3, {st_mode=S_IFREG|0755, st_size=2000480, ...}) = 0
mmap(NULL, 8192, PROT_READ|PROT_WRITE,
MAP_PRIVATE|MAP_ANONYMOUS, -1, 0) = 0x7fabec86e000
mmap(NULL, 2008696, PROT_READ, MAP_PRIVATE|MAP_DENYWRITE,
3, 0) = 0x7fabec683000
mmap(0x7fabec6a8000, 1519616, PROT_READ|PROT_EXEC,
MAP_PRIVATE|MAP_FIXED|MAP_DENYWRITE, 3, 0x25000) =
0x7fabec6a8000
mmap(0x7fabec81b000, 299008, PROT_READ,
MAP_PRIVATE|MAP_FIXED|MAP_DENYWRITE, 3, 0x198000) =
0x7fabec81b000
mmap(0x7fabec864000, 24576, PROT_READ|PROT_WRITE,
MAP_PRIVATE|MAP_FIXED|MAP_DENYWRITE, 3, 0x1e0000) =
0x7fabec864000
mmap(0x7fabec86a000, 13944, PROT_READ|PROT_WRITE,
MAP_PRIVATE|MAP_FIXED|MAP_ANONYMOUS, -1, 0) =
0x7fabec86a000
close(3)                                    = 0
arch_prctl(ARCH_SET_FS, 0x7fabec86f500) = 0
mprotect(0x7fabec864000, 12288, PROT_READ) = 0
mprotect(0x56225fe38000, 4096, PROT_READ) = 0
mprotect(0x7fabec8b0000, 4096, PROT_READ) = 0
munmap(0x7fabec870000, 89340)               = 0
openat(AT_FDCWD, "/mnt/a", O_RDWR|O_CREAT|O_APPEND|O_SYNC,
022530) = 3
write(3, "XXXXXXXXXXXXXXXXXXXX", 20)     = 20
close(3)                                    = 0
exit_group(0)                               = ?
+++ exited with 0 +++
```

Going through the output of the strace command, we find that the main "write" is performed by the "write()" system call. This is where the journey of the I/O begins. Let us dive into this "write()" system call.

Filesystem Implementation

Filesystem is a way to store files in a raw disk. Raw disk is a linear collection of sectors. There are different names for sectors, such as disk block number (DBN), Logical block addresses (LBA).

Why can't applications write to raw disks directly; that way we can avoid the filesystem and perhaps decrease latency?

Applications can write to raw disk, but there are implications of that. Say if an application assumes that each 512-byte sector is a file. Then it can write to every sector assuming that it is a file. Limitations of this approach is that the application cannot make files greater than 512 bytes. This approach will not allow the Application to store any metadata related to the file either. The application will not be able to store the last accessed times for each file, the file name, etc.

Another question that might arise is, why is a layered approach to addressing is needed, where applications work on virtual addresses, and they are converted on the fly to physical addresses.

This approach has a number of advantages.
1) Fragmentation on the physical address space is avoided.
2) Applications do not have a view of the physical address space.
3) The memory space on which the applications operate looks contiguous.
4) Efficient utilization of memory.

Because of these reasons there has to be a structured way to store and retrieve data from the disk. The solution to the structured reads/writes to a disk is a filesystem. A filesystem provides functionalities of space management, filenames, directories and metadata.

Because of the features provided by the filesystem, the filesystems store data in the file block numbers. The filesystem knows that an I/O meant for a particular file block number corresponds to which disk block. The mapping from file block number to disk block number is managed by the filesystem itself. This mapping can be kept in a file block table or B+ trees etc.

We will see a sample UNIX filesystem mapping which uses the Inode structure. While making this type of mapping care was taken to ensure that least disk accesses shall be performed to reach from an Inode index to the actual disk block. All the pointers are stored in the Inode table. The initial pointers to the disk blocks are a one to one mapping. These are called the direct pointers.

Now If we have all the direct pointers then the number of pointers will increase drastically for big files.
Hence they came up with double indirect and triple indirect blocks.

These type of addresses are depicted in the following diagram :

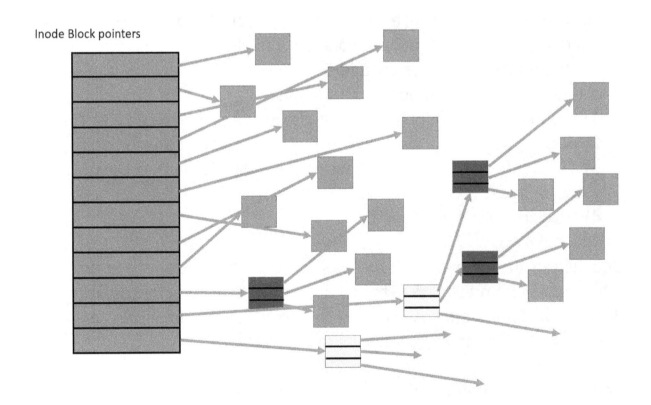

Inode Block pointers

In the above diagram, the green blocks indicate directly addressed blocks, whereas the purple and yellow blocks indicate double and triple indirect blocks respectively.

EXT4 block disk layout

In ext4, the file to logical block map has been replaced with an extent tree. Under the old scheme, allocating a contiguous run of 1,000 blocks required an indirect block to map all 1,000 entries; with extents, the mapping is reduced to a single "struct ext4_extent" with ee_len = 1000.

```
crash>  struct ext4_extent
struct ext4_extent {
    __le32 ee_block;
    __le16 ee_len;
    __le16 ee_start_hi;
    __le32 ee_start_lo;
}
```

SIZE: 12 bytes

The I/O journey

System call

When we take a look at the implementation of the "write()" system call, we see that it just calls the function "ksys_write()" with the same parameters as "write()".

```
SYSCALL_DEFINE3(write, unsigned int, fd, const char __user
*, buf,
    size_t, count)
{
    return ksys_write(fd, buf, count);
}
```

The above code uses the macro "SYSCALL_DEFINE3" to define the system call "write()". The number 3 in the macro is the number of parameters that the system call uses. Hence for a system call like "fstat()", or "kill()" the macro "SYSCALL_DEFINE2" is used.

The macro "SYSCALL_DEFINE3" expands to "SYSCALL_DEFINEx", which expands to 2 macros.

```
#define SYSCALL_DEFINEx(x, sname, ...)                        \
    SYSCALL_METADATA(sname, x, __VA_ARGS__)                   \
    __SYSCALL_DEFINEx(x, sname, __VA_ARGS__)
```

The code in the macro "SYSCALL_METADATA" runs only when the macro "CONFIG_FTRACE_SYSCALLS" is defined and is used to define metadata for tracing purposes.

The macro "__SYSCALL_DEFINEx" expands to the code which actually defines the system call. We will not discuss the details since it is not under the scope of this chapter.

The function "ksys_write()" checks whether the file descriptor passed to it valid or not, and calls the function "vfs_write()"

```
ssize_t ksys_write(unsigned int fd, const char __user *buf,
size_t count)
{
.

    if (f.file) {
    loff_t pos = file_pos_read(f.file);
        ret = vfs_write(f.file, buf, count, &pos);

.

}
```

With this function call, the I/O has entered the VFS layer of the IO stack.

The VFS layer

VFS stands for Virtual File System. The VFS layer provides a common set of interfaces for all the filesystems. Each filesystem defines its own VFS style functions. The VFS functions are all defined using the structure "file_operations".

The "file_operations" structure looks like this :

```
struct file_operations {
    struct module *owner;
    loff_t (*llseek) (struct file *, loff_t, int);
    ssize_t (*read) (struct file *, char __user *, size_t,
loff_t *);
    ssize_t (*write) (struct file *, const char __user *,
size_t, loff_t *);
    ssize_t (*read_iter) (struct kiocb *, struct iov_iter
*);
    ssize_t (*write_iter) (struct kiocb *, struct iov_iter
*);
    int (*iterate) (struct file *, struct dir_context *);
    int (*iterate_shared) (struct file *, struct
dir_context *);
    __poll_t (*poll) (struct file *, struct
poll_table_struct *);
    long (*unlocked_ioctl) (struct file *, unsigned int,
unsigned long);
    long (*compat_ioctl) (struct file *, unsigned int,
unsigned long);
    int (*mmap) (struct file *, struct vm_area_struct *);
    unsigned long mmap_supported_flags;
    int (*open) (struct inode *, struct file *);
    int (*flush) (struct file *, fl_owner_t id);
    int (*release) (struct inode *, struct file *);
    int (*fsync) (struct file *, loff_t, loff_t, int
datasync);
    int (*fasync) (int, struct file *, int);
    int (*lock) (struct file *, int, struct file_lock *);
```

```
    ssize_t (*sendpage) (struct file *, struct page *, int,
size_t, loff_t *, int);
    unsigned long (*get_unmapped_area)(struct file *,
unsigned long, unsigned long, unsigned long, unsigned
long);
    int (*check_flags)(int);
    int (*flock) (struct file *, int, struct file_lock *);
    ssize_t (*splice_write)(struct pipe_inode_info *,
struct file *, loff_t *, size_t, unsigned int);
    ssize_t (*splice_read)(struct file *, loff_t *, struct
pipe_inode_info *, size_t, unsigned int);
    int (*setlease)(struct file *, long, struct file_lock
**, void **);
    long (*fallocate)(struct file *file, int mode, loff_t
offset,
              loff_t len);
    void (*show_fdinfo)(struct seq_file *m, struct file
*f);
#ifndef CONFIG_MMU
    unsigned (*mmap_capabilities)(struct file *);
#endif
    ssize_t (*copy_file_range)(struct file *, loff_t,
struct file *,
            loff_t, size_t, unsigned int);
    loff_t (*remap_file_range)(struct file *file_in, loff_t
pos_in,
                  struct file *file_out, loff_t pos_out,
                  loff_t len, unsigned int remap_flags);
    int (*fadvise)(struct file *, loff_t, loff_t, int);
} __randomize_layout;
```

The following diagram depicts the VFS layer

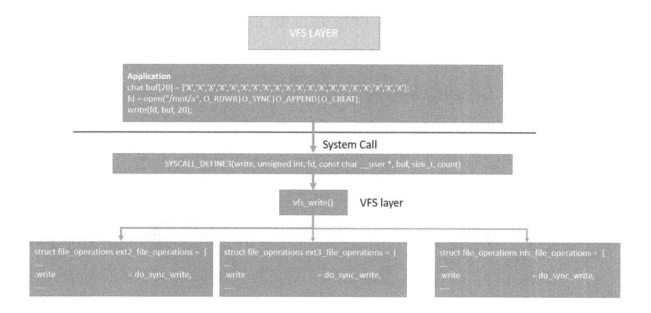

Each file system must define these function pointers. The implementation for the common interface is done by each file system.

If we see the kernel/fs directory we see that all the filesystem specific folders are present. For this example, we are using the ext4 filesystem.

Let us get back to our function "vfs_write()". The function "vfs_write()" first verifies whether the read/write area to which the write is issued to, is valid or not. It then calls the function "__vfs_write()". We can observe that the "file_operations" function pointers are being used here (and will be used later too).

```
ssize_t __vfs_write(struct file *file, const char __user
*p, size_t count,
        loff_t *pos)
{
    if (file->f_op->write)
        return file->f_op->write(file, p, count, pos);
    else if (file->f_op->write_iter)
        return new_sync_write(file, p, count, pos);
    else
    return -EINVAL;
}
```

Since the ext4 filesystem does not have an implementation of the ".write" function (see ext4_file_operations structure) , the code calls the function "new_sync_write()".

The "new_sync_write()" function first creates an "iovec" structure out of the buffer and the length provided to the "write()" system call.

```
static ssize_t new_sync_write(struct file *filp, const char
__user *buf, size_t len, loff_t *ppos)
{
     struct iovec iov = { .iov_base = (void __user *)buf,
.iov_len = len };
     .

     .


          iov_iter_init(&iter, WRITE, &iov, 1, len);

     ret = call_write_iter(filp, &kiocb, &iter);

     .

}
```

This buffer ("buf") contains the array of characters which is supposed to be written to the file and the "len" contains the number of characters to be written, which translates to number of bytes in case of ASCII encoding. This "iovec" structure is used to initialize an "iov_iter" structure, which is then passed on to the function "call_write_iter()". Here the "kiocb" structure is also created and passed to "call_write_iter()", which will be used later. The function "call_write_iter()" simply calls the function pointed out by the file_operations function pointer ".write_iter".

```
static inline ssize_t call_write_iter(struct file *file,
struct kiocb *kio,
                    struct iov_iter *iter)
{
     return file->f_op->write_iter(kio, iter);
}
```

For an ext4 filesystem, ".write_iter" points to the function "ext4_file_write_iter()".

The function "ext4_file_write_iter()" first checks whether the file is associated with DAX or not. DAX stands for direct access, which is the part of the code added for persistent memory support. One of the ways to access persistent memories is to memory map files to that memory region and use it with general read/write system calls. If the file to which this "write()" was aimed at was memory mapped to a persistent memory area, then the code would take this route.

```
static ssize_t
ext4_file_write_iter(struct kiocb *iocb, struct iov_iter
*from)
{
.
#ifdef CONFIG_FS_DAX
    if (IS_DAX(inode))
    return ext4_dax_write_iter(iocb, from);
.
ret = ext4_write_checks(iocb, from);
.

.
ret = __generic_file_write_iter(iocb, from);
.
 if (ret > 0)
        ret = generic_write_sync(iocb, ret);
.
}
```

The function then performs a number of checks through the function "ext4_write_checks()". Checks performed include whether the write size is bigger than the size of the file allowed in the system (using RLIMIT_FSIZE macro), basic access checks, etc.

At this point let us stop for a while and understand the high-level division of stages through which an I/O goes. This will also help us immensely in understanding the code flow later on in this chapter.

When data is to be written to a file, it does not get written to the disk directly, where the file actually resides, instead the data is first written to an intermediate layer called the buffer cache, or page cache as it is called nowadays. And for most writes, the system call returns from here (if "O_SYNC" flag is not used). Later, in the background, the buffers (or pages) which have been written to (let's call them dirty pages), are written to their corresponding blocks in the file residing on the disk.

In the latest kernels, the above mentioned background task is again divided into two steps, or I should say layers. The first one fetches the dirty pages which are to be written to the disk, and the second one performs the write according to the underlying protocol (SCSI in most cases). The second layer is called the multi-queue block layer.

Now let us get back to the code execution path. The function "__generic_file_write_iter()", which is called next takes care of two things, direct write IO path and running the page cache code. Direct I/O path means that the data is written directly to the disk and the page cache is skipped. Page cache on the other hand will (as discussed earlier), update the data in the cache, mark the pages written as dirty. Now, the job of writing those dirty pages to the disk is completed by the next layer. We will not delve deep into the page cache code path in this chapter.

At this point we have to understand that the page cache code would have updated the "iocb" structure in the function "ext4_file_write_iter()". This structure would contain the start and end markers, which would help the next layer pick up dirty pages.

Let us take a look at the stack trace of the next layer, which is where the dirty pages are obtained, and "bio" structures are created and sent to the multi-queue (MQ) block layer.

```
kernel: [ 4172.841177]   ? submit_bio+0x5/0x160
kernel: [ 4172.841178]   ? ext4_io_submit+0x4d/0x60
kernel: [ 4172.841179]   ? submit_bio+0x5/0x160
kernel: [ 4172.841181]   ? ext4_io_submit+0x4d/0x60
kernel: [ 4172.841182]   ext4_writepages+0x3f5/0x950
kernel: [ 4172.841186]   do_writepages+0x43/0xd0
kernel:          [        4172.841187]                    ?
mpage_map_and_submit_extent+0x4a0/0x4a0
kernel: [ 4172.841188]   ? do_writepages+0x43/0xd0
kernel:                  [                          4172.841190]
__filemap_fdatawrite_range+0xd5/0x110
kernel: [ 4172.841192]   file_write_and_wait_range+0x5a/0xb0
kernel: [ 4172.841194]   ext4_sync_file+0x8f/0x3e0
kernel: [ 4172.841196]   vfs_fsync_range+0x49/0x80
kernel: [ 4172.841197]   ext4_file_write_iter+0x103/0x3b0
kernel: [ 4172.841200]   new_sync_write+0x125/0x1c0
kernel: [ 4172.841202]   __vfs_write+0x29/0x40
kernel: [ 4172.841203]   vfs_write+0xb9/0x1a0
kernel: [ 4172.841205]   ksys_write+0x67/0xe0
kernel: [ 4172.841206]   __x64_sys_write+0x1a/0x20
kernel: [ 4172.841208]   do_syscall_64+0x5a/0x130
kernel:                  [                          4172.841210]
entry_SYSCALL_64_after_hwframe+0x44/0xa9
```

In the above trace we can spot the function "ext4_file_write_iter()" where we are at this point. Here, we have the "iocb" structure which holds the page markers and the inode structure of the file. The function "ext4_file_write_iter()" calls "generic_write_sync()" function, which is an inline function (hence not visible in the trace above). It checks the "O_SYNC" flag and calls "vfs_fsync_range()" accordingly, with the start and end page markers from "iocb".

```
static inline ssize_t generic_write_sync(struct kiocb *iocb,
ssize_t count)
{
    if (iocb->ki_flags & IOCB_DSYNC) {
     int ret = vfs_fsync_range(iocb->ki_filp,
```

```
       iocb->ki_pos - count, iocb->ki_pos - 1,
       (iocb->ki_flags & IOCB_SYNC) ? 0 : 1);
```

The "vfs_fsync_range()" function simply uses the ".fsync" function pointer and calls the function "ext4_sync_file()" (since in our example we are using the ext4 filesystem). The function "ext4_sync_file()" calls "__generic_file_fsync()" if journaling is not on. We will not discuss journaling in this chapter for the time being.

After that the execution goes through the functions "file_write_and_wait_range()" -> "__filemap_fdatawrite_range()" -> "do_writepages()". The function "do_writepages()" checks whether the address space operation function pointer ".writepages" has been defined or not. For ext4 filesystems, the ".writepages" pointer would be pointing to the function "ext4_writepages()".

```
int do_writepages(struct address_space *mapping, struct
writeback_control *wbc)
{
.
.

    if (mapping->a_ops->writepages)
            ret = mapping->a_ops->writepages(mapping, wbc);
.
}
```

The function "ext4_writepages()" performs a number of small steps, and a few big ones. Among the big ones, there is something called "plugging" and "unplugging" that it does.

```
static int ext4_writepages(struct address_space *mapping,
            struct writeback_control *wbc)
{
.
.

    blk_start_plug(&plug);
```

```
    ret = mpage_prepare_extent_to_map(&mpd);
     /* Submit prepared bio */
    ext4_io_submit(&mpd.io_submit);
    ext4_put_io_end_defer(mpd.io_submit.io_end);


    while (!done && mpd.first_page <= mpd.last_page) {

        ret = mpage_prepare_extent_to_map(&mpd);
    if (!ret) {
        if (mpd.map.m_len)
                ret  =  mpage_map_and_submit_extent(handle,
&mpd,
                &give_up_on_write);


        ext4_io_submit(&mpd.io_submit);

unplug:
    blk_finish_plug(&plug);

}
```

The "ext4_writepages()" function uses the "mpage_*" functions, the start and end page markers from the page cache and the inode address mapping to fetch the dirty pages and store them in the "mpd.io_submit" structure. This structure is of the type "struct ext4_io_submit" which holds the "bio" structure. The "bio" structure is the main unit of I/O for the block layer and lower layers. All of this is done while plugging is enabled, as marked by the functions "blk_*_plug()".

This plugging concept enables the lower layer to merge related and nearby I/Os, and batch them into single requests for increased efficiency. As you can see, the passing of the IOs to MQ block layer is done while plugging is enabled. We will see how this is used later when we discuss the MQ block layer.

Next the "ext4_io_submit()" function calls "submit_bio() function. The function "submit_bio()" is the last function in this layer. It calls the function "generic_make_request()", which marks the starting of the MQ block layer.

Multi-queue block layer

Long time ago, (in a galaxy far far away), the Linux block layer had a single path of IO submission and completion. This presented a bottleneck for modern systems with multi-core CPUs and fast SSDs storage. To tackle this problem a multi queue block layer was introduced. This layer relies on two sets of queues, software and hardware queues. Software queues which are used for I/O submission and are typically equal to the number of CPUs in the system. Hardware queues are used to submit the I/Os to the underlying device (SSD, HDD, logical volume). The number of these typically depend on the underlying device.

The following diagram depicts the layout of the queues in the MQBL.

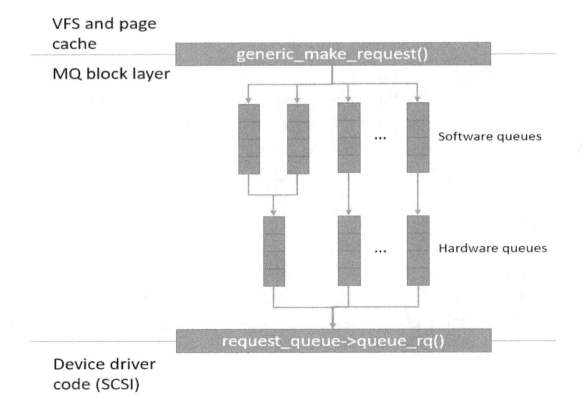

The MQ block layer (MQBL) is designed in a way which allows any device driver (typically IO) code to hook in to its API and start using the queue submission and completion mechanism. There are a number of simple steps which are to be followed to use the MQBL. There are obviously ways to fine tune and configure the parameters as required. We will look into the simple way of hooking in to the MQBL code. This will also help us in understanding the I/O flow.

Let us look into the initial steps involved in using the MQ block layer, along with the important data structures.

1. The MQBL initialization API uses the structure "blk_mq_tag_set" for initialization. This structure is a way of communicating your custom driver related information to the MQBL. It contains information about the number of hardware and software queues, command size, and so on. It also contains a pointer to the structure "blk_mq_ops", which contains function pointers to your custom function which will be called from the MQBL code. Out of these functions, the essential ones which you must define are "queue_rq_fn" (used to submit the command to your underlying device) and "map_queues_fn" (used to map the software queues to the hardware queues).
   Once the "blk_mq_tag_set" is set with the relevant data, the function "blk_mq_alloc_tag_set()" is called with the structure.

2. The second step is to initialize the "request_queue" structure, which is one of the main structures in the MQBL. It will be used internally by the MQBL to access the custom function pointers. Besides that, it holds a lot of MQBL related data fields.
   To initialize the "request_queue", the function "blk_mq_init_queue()" is used, and the "blk_mq_tag_set" structure is sent to it. This also sets the "make_request_structure" of the "request_queue" to "blk_mq_make_request()".

Now let us get back to our I/O journey. In the last section, we saw that the MQBL was entered by calling the function "generic_make_request()", we will pick it up from there. Let us take a look at the trace of the I/O from here.

```
kernel: [ 1664.030503]  ? scsi_init_command+0x150/0x150
kernel: [ 1664.030505]  ? scsi_queue_rq+0x5/0x9b0
kernel: [ 1664.030506]  ?
blk_mq_dispatch_rq_list+0x97/0x540
kernel: [ 1664.030507]  ? scsi_queue_rq+0x5/0x9b0
kernel: [ 1664.030508]  ?
blk_mq_dispatch_rq_list+0x97/0x540
kernel: [ 1664.030509]  ? deadline_remove_request+0x4e/0xb0
kernel: [ 1664.030511]  ? dd_dispatch_request+0x1/0x1f0
kernel: [ 1664.030513]  blk_mq_do_dispatch_sched+0x67/0x100
kernel: [ 1664.030514]
blk_mq_sched_dispatch_requests+0x12d/0x180
kernel: [ 1664.030516]  __blk_mq_run_hw_queue+0x5a/0x110
kernel: [ 1664.030517]
__blk_mq_delay_run_hw_queue+0x15b/0x160
kernel: [ 1664.030519]  blk_mq_run_hw_queue+0x92/0x120
kernel: [ 1664.030520]
blk_mq_sched_insert_requests+0x74/0x100
kernel: [ 1664.030522]  blk_mq_flush_plug_list+0x1e8/0x290
kernel: [ 1664.030523]  ? generic_make_request+0xcf/0x320
```

The function "generic_make_request()" first extracts the "request_queue" from the disk structure. It then iterates over the bios (sent now and previously) and calls the "make_request_function" of the "request_queue", which is "blk_mq_make_request()". There is a lot more happening inside "generic_make_request()" (like having two different lists of bios, one for current function call, and one for the previous ones), but we will not delve into the details here.

```
blk_qc_t generic_make_request(struct bio *bio)
{
.
    struct request_queue *q = bio->bi_disk->queue;
.
    do {
            ret = q->make_request_fn(q, bio);
```

```
        bio = bio_list_pop(&bio_list_on_stack[0]);
    } while (bio);
}
```

The function "blk_mq_make_request()" has several paths, but the one we will look into is the one which is taken when plugging is enabled and there is only a single hardware queue (SCSI probably). It is safe to say that most of the other paths also lead to scheduler code. In this function the bio is transformed into the "request" structure.

When plugging is on, for a "request", the function "blk_mq_make_request()" checks if the number of "request"s (I/O) waiting in the plug has crossed the BLK_MAX_REQUEST_COUNT. If it has, then the function **blk_flush_plug_list()"** is called to flush the "request"s to the scheduler, otherwise, the "request" is added to the plug.

```
static blk_qc_t blk_mq_make_request(struct request_queue
*q, struct bio *bio)
{
    .

    else if (plug && (q->nr_hw_queues == 1 || q->mq_ops-
>commit_rqs)) {
        .

        if (request_count >= BLK_MAX_REQUEST_COUNT || (last
&&

                blk_rq_bytes(last) >= BLK_PLUG_FLUSH_SIZE)) {
            blk_flush_plug_list(plug, false);
            trace_block_plug(q);
        }

        blk_add_rq_to_plug(plug, rq);
    }

    .

}
```

After that the code execution path is "blk_flush_plug_list()" -> "blk_mq_flush_plug_list()" -> "blk_mq_sched_insert_requests()". We can observe "blk_mq_sched_insert_requests()" in the trace we posted earlier.

The function "blk_mq_sched_insert_requests()" extracts the "elevator_queue" structure from the "request_queue" structure and uses that to insert the "request" into the scheduler. The Linux kernel has a number of scheduling algorithms to choose from.

Some of the IO scheduling algorithms are,
"Deadline," "CFQ (Complete Fairness Queueing)," and "Noop (No Operation)."

One can check which scheduling algorithm its Linux system is using by running the following command.

```
# cat /sys/block/sda/queue/scheduler
[mq-deadline] none
```
The function then calls "blk_mq_run_hw_queue()", to start executing the "request"s from the scheduler.

From here onwards the scheduler code starts.

```
kernel: [ 1664.030507]  ? scsi_queue_rq+0x5/0x9b0
kernel: [ 1664.030508]  ?
blk_mq_dispatch_rq_list+0x97/0x540
kernel: [ 1664.030509]  ? deadline_remove_request+0x4e/0xb0
kernel: [ 1664.030511]  ? dd_dispatch_request+0x1/0x1f0
kernel: [ 1664.030513]  blk_mq_do_dispatch_sched+0x67/0x100
kernel: [ 1664.030514]
blk_mq_sched_dispatch_requests+0x12d/0x180
kernel: [ 1664.030516]  __blk_mq_run_hw_queue+0x5a/0x110
kernel: [ 1664.030517]
 __blk_mq_delay_run_hw_queue+0x15b/0x160
kernel: [ 1664.030519]  blk_mq_run_hw_queue+0x92/0x120
```

The trace above shows the code execution path of the scheduler.

Since our block device was using the default "deadline" scheduler, the function "dd_dispatch_request()" is called. These details are all stored in the "elevator_queue" structure. The reader is encouraged to read about the different schedulers.

The function blk_mq_dispatch_rq_list() is the last function in the MQBL layer. It extracts the "request" containing the I/O and creates a "blk_mq_queue_data" structure from it. It then uses the "blk_mq_ops" structure from the "request_queue" structure, and calls the "queue_rq" function. This "queue_rq" is the same function pointer which was set during the initialization of the MQBL.

```
bool blk_mq_dispatch_rq_list(struct request_queue *q, struct
list_head *list,
                bool got_budget)
{
.
.

    do {
     struct blk_mq_queue_data bd;
.
.
     bd.rq = rq;
.
.
        ret = q->mq_ops->queue_rq(hctx, &bd);
}
```

SCSI Layer

Since the above trace is for a SCSI device, the "queue_rq" points to the function "scsi_queue_rq()". The function extracts the "request" from the "blk_mq_queue_data" structure and creates a SCSI command out of it. It then updates the "scsi_done" pointer for the command, and makes it point to the function "scsi_mq_done(). This will be called by the device when the

command execution is completed. Lastly, the function scsi_dispatch_cmd()"
is called to dispatch the command.

```
static    blk_status_t    scsi_queue_rq(struct    blk_mq_hw_ctx
*hctx,
          const struct blk_mq_queue_data *bd)
{
    struct request *req = bd->rq;
        struct request_queue *q = req->q;
    struct scsi_device *sdev = q->queuedata;
    struct Scsi_Host *shost = sdev->host;
    struct scsi_cmnd *cmd = blk_mq_rq_to_pdu(req);

    .

    cmd->scsi_done = scsi_mq_done;

    reason = scsi_dispatch_cmd(cmd);

    .

}
```

The function "scsi_dispatch_cmd()" finally uses the driver code to queue the
command. The SCSI command is queued to the lower level device driver.

Lower layer Device driver

SCSI dispatch calls lower level device driver's queuecommand function.
This is illustrated here:

```
static int scsi_dispatch_cmd(struct scsi_cmnd *cmd)
{
    .

    rtn = host->hostt->queuecommand(host, cmd);

    .

}
```

This ".queuecommand" pointer would point to the SCSI driver function which
the underlying device is using.

In Linux queuecommand function is defined by various lower level drivers:

1 iscsi_iser.c   <global>   =   scsi_991   .queuecommand   = **iscsi_queuecommand**,

2 ib_srp.c <global>   3287 .queuecommand = srp_queuecommand,

3 mptfc.c <global>   114 .queuecommand = mptfc_qcmd,

4 mptsas.c <global>   1978 .queuecommand = **mptsas_qcmd**,

...

a fcoe.c   <global>   279 .queuecommand = fc_queuecommand,

7 init.c   <global>   155   .queuecommand   = sas_queuecommand,

8 iscsi_tcp.c   <global>   977   .queuecommand   = iscsi_queuecommand,

9 lpfc_scsi.c   <global>   6126   .queuecommand   = lpfc_no_command,

a lpfc_scsi.c   <global>   6149   .queuecommand   = **lpfc_queuecommand**,

We see that several drivers like iscsi, mptsas, fibre channel, sas and emulex HBA define queuecommand function.

After queueing the command, the code returns from here.

Return from Lower level device driver

The completion is called by the driver through the "scsi_done" pointer set in the command. This calls "scsi_mq_done()" for SCSI devices.

The function execution sequence from here is "scsi_mq_done() -> blk_mq_complete_request() -> __blk_mq_complete_request()".

The function "__blk_mq_complete_request()" calls "__blk_complete_request()" (since we have just one hardware queue in our case). A soft IRQ (BLOCK_SOFTIRQ) is raised in the function "__blk_complete_request()", which triggers the function "blk_done_softirq()". The function "blk_done_softirq()" uses the "blk_mq_ops" structure from the "request_queue" structure, and calls the ".complete" pointer, which points to "scsi_softirq_done()" for SCSI devices.

```
kernel: [ 2317.943329]   ? blk_mq_free_request+0x5/0x100
kernel: [ 2317.943330]   ? __blk_mq_end_request+0x114/0x120
kernel: [ 2317.943330]   ? blk_mq_free_request+0x5/0x100
kernel: [ 2317.943331]   ? __blk_mq_end_request+0x114/0x120
kernel: [ 2317.943333]   scsi_end_request+0xa7/0x160
kernel: [ 2317.943335]   scsi_io_completion+0x7c/0x540
kernel: [ 2317.943336]   ? smp_apic_timer_interrupt+0x7b/0x140
kernel: [ 2317.943337]   scsi_finish_command+0xe7/0x120
kernel: [ 2317.943339]   scsi_softirq_done+0x14a/0x170
kernel: [ 2317.943340]   blk_done_softirq+0x92/0xc0
```

The function execution sequence after this is "scsi_softirq_done() -> scsi_finish_command() -> scsi_io_completion() -> scsi_end_request() -> __blk_mq_end_request()".

A number of things are done in this sequence of function execution. Flags are cleared which allows the device to accept new commands. It handles support for bidirectional commands.

This path, at the end, completes and frees the request.

Complete Linux IO stack

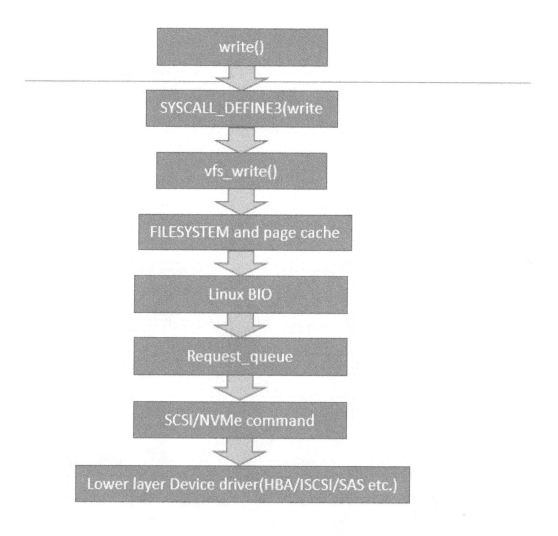